MOVING PANELS

TRANSLATING COMICS TO FILM

MOVING PANELS

TRANSLATING COMICS TO FILM

LOGAN LUDWIG

Sᴇǫᴜᴀʀᴛ Oʀɢᴀɴɪᴢᴀᴛɪᴏɴ   Eᴅᴡᴀʀᴅꜱᴠɪʟʟᴇ, Iʟʟɪɴᴏɪꜱ

Moving Panels: Translating Comics to Film
by Logan Ludwig

First edition, Feb 2015, ISBN 978-1-9405-8909-1.

Cover by Jeffrey Vincent Stong. Design by Julian Darius. Interior art is © various creators and companies.

Published by Sequart Organization. Edited by Hannah Means-Shannon. Assistant edited by Stuart Warren, Glen Downey, Julian Darius, and Mike Phillips. Thanks to Alyssa Warren, Nicolas Labarre, Henry Northmore, Chris Rywalt, M. S. Wilson, and Patrick Wilson.

For more information about other titles in this series, visit Sequart.org/books.

Contents

Previously...

The film industry can't seem to stop adapting comic books. Studios are hooked on trying to find the next big franchise, and comics seem to be their current bet for box office success. Whether it's long-running series featuring characters such as Batman or Spider-Man, new comic properties, or even comics that haven't been released yet (for instance, the film version of *Kick-Ass* was in production before the comic had wrapped its first mini-series), sequential storytelling offers filmmakers a well of ideas ready-made for translation to the big screen. The trend doesn't seem likely to slow down, and the film industry will continue scouring the comic world for more material for years to come.

Not only is Hollywood taking comic properties and turning them into films, but there's also a growing trend of creators crossing from one medium to the other. Writer-directors like Joss Whedon are dabbling in comics more frequently, while also taking charge of cinematic mega-properties such as *The Avengers*. Conversely, comic creators like Mark Millar are being brought in by studios such as 20th Century-Fox to oversee their comic-book adaptations. Because of this, it's important to ask ourselves how closely related the two media are and just how easy it is to move from comics to film. But are comics as natural a fit for translation to the screen as Hollywood seems to believe?

This book examines how disparate these two media are, proving that comics are more than storyboards for films without budgets. Each medium possess unique qualities in terms of its storytelling capabilities, but the two are also similar in form. Neither is better, neither is worse. Each simply operates by certain rules that shape how the creator approaches the project. Creators moving from one of these media to the other might have a slight advantage over other creators, but any such move requires the creator to adapt to their new medium—to learn new and varied techniques so they can tell their stories in the most effective fashion possible.

In examining the relationship between these two forms of media, it's useful to focus on adaptation, in which the "same" story is told in both media. The differences in these tellings often reflect the differences between the media themselves, and by examining these adaptations we may come to better understand the differences between comics and film.

Fidelity and *Watchmen*

This raises an important issue: the notion of fidelity. For the purposes of this book, "fidelity" will mean creating equivalent, rather than identical, effects across the different media. Fidelity is not a literal translation of images and content, which is always adapted. Current attitudes toward adapting comics to film tend to privilege superficial forms of fidelity. One need only look at the film version of *Watchmen*, one of the most important comics of all time.

In the words of Jeffrey Dean Morgan, the actor who portrays the Comedian in the film: "It's so true to the book I can't even begin to tell you how. Everything is so true to the book it's insane. You can put anything that has been built for *Watchmen* next to a panel in the book and it'll trip you out. It's amazing."[1] While Morgan's assessment may be correct (the movie does emulate the comic's look), it misses a crucial reason why the original work looked the way it did. Alan Moore and Dave Gibbons designed *Watchmen* to evoke classic comic-book aesthetics, so their choices for the book's design, such as color, built upon the visual history of comics. *Watchmen* was a book built on the history of the medium and, for readers steeped in comics, this creates a subtext for the work that comments on the story and its relation to other stories that preceded it. When the film version of *Watchmen* copies this visual style exactly, this comics-specific subtext breaks down. Mainstream filmgoers are not expected to have a working knowledge of the history of comic-book

---

[1] Topel, Fred. "Jeffrey Dean Morgan Says *Watchmen*'s Comedian Lives Up to the Book." 2007. rottentomatoes.com/m/watchmen/news/1697905/jeffrey_dean_morgan_says_watchmens_comedian_lives_up_to_the_book (accessed 27 Oct 2008).

aesthetics. Because of this decision to be faithful to the original work, the film's direction interferes with the intent and purpose of Moore's design.

Couldn't the film have replicated aesthetic traditions from previous film adaptations of super-hero comics? While some attempts have been made to accomplish this (e.g. the rubbery costume redesigns evoke some '90s super-hero films such as Joel Schumacher's *Batman and Robin*), the movie is largely content with reproducing the original work on the screen. *Watchmen*, on the other hand, draws on a variety of aesthetic and storytelling norms that have been built up over decades of comics and their history rather than just the relatively small footprint of comic-book films. Moore and Gibbons's *Watchmen* is more than just a simple story: it's a commentary on the medium as a whole. Adapting this material to a different medium can feel essentially pointless. Brian K. Vaughan, a writer who works in comics, television, and film, put it simply: "it's like making a stage play of *Citizen Kane*. I guess it could be OK, but why? The medium is the message."[2] The film ends up failing simply because it is too slavishly faithful to its source, and in doing so it loses sight of what made the original comic so provocative and effective.

Admittedly, *Watchmen* is an extreme example, and it's quite rare for any work to be so strongly tied to its original medium. Still, it's a useful case study because it helps highlight the issue that no matter how close two media may seem, they are inevitably unique in both their storytelling capacities and their aesthetic histories. Adapting *Watchmen* is a thankless task, because the story and its meaning are inherently tied to comics as a medium.

I'll explore *Watchmen* specifically in a later chapter. For the moment, it's useful to step back and deal with some larger, more theoretical issues.

Understanding Comics Adaptation

I'd now like to look into the issue of adapting material between media. I intend to deploy a variety of case studies to help explain how comics and films function and what similarities and differences arise when telling stories. These case studies will be wide-ranging and focus on a variety of topics and works, from the mainstream super-hero stories featured in *Iron Man* and *The Invincible Iron Man* to the autobiographical comic and film versions of Marjane Satrapi's

---

[2] Rogers, Adam. *Filming the Unfilmable: Behind the Scenes of the Watchmen Movie.* 2009. www.wired.com/entertainment/hollywood/magazine/17-03/ff_watchman?currentPage=all (accessed 15 Mar 2009).

Persepolis. These aesthetic studies will help us focus on some of the unique capabilities of comics and films and make a strong case for recognizing comics as a singular medium with capabilities unlike any other.

We must take a step back and look at the scholarly work that already exists in relation to comics. Much has been written about film and its aesthetic qualities, but when it comes to comics there is a much smaller body of work to dig into. There are "how-to" books and histories of comics, but there is significantly less writing devoted to serious aesthetic discussions of comics. We must establish a base from which to work before heading further. By and large, current comic-book criticism deals with comic content as opposed to the form. While there are many critics who understand how comics function, this is of less interest to those interpreting what comics "mean" in a more traditional, literary sense. Symbolism and metaphors have come to the front in many critical essays, but still, a more robust formal discussion of aesthetics demands inquiry.

This style of literary comic criticism is exemplified by Douglas Wolk's work in his book *Reading Comics: How Graphic Novels Work and What They Mean*. Wolk tackles larger issues that seem to interest him more than actually engaging with how comics work; to say his book is weighted toward the "What They Mean" side of his title is an understatement. Wolk states,

> Comics are not prose. Comics are not movies. They are not a text-driven medium with added pictures; they're not the visual equivalent of prose narrative or a static version of film. They are their own thing: a medium with its own devices, its own innovators, its own clichés, its own genres and traps and liberties.[3]

While I agree with Wolk's assertion, his book doesn't prove this fact. *Reading Comics* deals with interpretations of his favorite artists' works or lists of things he loves about comics. There are certainly useful moments here and there, when Wolk will break down a page layout and discuss how the reader moves his eyes through it and comprehends comics, but such analyses are few and far between. Wolk's work is not especially useful in developing an understanding of comic-book aesthetics and the rules that govern them. Also, since Wolk is interested only in comics, there is a lack of writing about how comics relate to other media, something that Will Eisner and Scott McCloud, author of *Understanding Comics: The Invisible Art* and *Making Comics: Storytelling Secrets*

---

[3] Wolk, Douglas. *Reading Comics: How Graphic Novels Work and What They Mean*. Cambridge, MA: Da Capo Press, 2007. Page 14.

of Comics, Manga and Graphic Novels, both talk about—even if they do not devote large portions of their work to this comparison.

McCloud's first major work on comics, *Understanding Comics*, is a strong step in the right direction that deals more with comics as a medium. But in the end, this book tends to skew toward a big-picture view of comics and focuses on large-scale theories rather than small details. He also prefers very specific labeling of the techniques that he describes, breaking down and defining comics in ways that are semantically rigid, if one accepts his definitions. Most of the time, this isn't a problem, since McCloud's ideas are generally sound and well-reasoned, but some of his ideas feel a bit restrictive. For example, McCloud's definition of "comics" reads as follows: "Juxtaposed pictorial and other images in deliberate sequence, intended to convey information and / or to produce an aesthetic response in the viewer."[4] While a good definition of comics, this leaves out one area that McCloud is slightly biased against: single-panel comics. These comics, such as *The Family Circus*, simply do not fit McCloud's definition, and this speaks to how McCloud views the medium.

The main reason I object to this definition of comics is that the manipulation of the static image is equally important to comics as the way the medium juxtaposes images against one another. In a comic, a single character can exist within one panel multiple times, denoting the passage of time. Their movement can be marked, à la *The Family Circus's* predilection for charting out the path of a character with overly intricate dotted lines, or a single image can be broken down with small borders to simulate forward movement. Simply adding a word balloon to a panel adds the dimension of time without the need for a juxtaposition of images. Ultimately, these manipulations of time in an otherwise static image are just as important to the medium as the juxtaposition of images in succession.

In terms of McCloud's overall work, his focus on the sequential nature of comics and other large-scale issues causes him to spend less time with the smaller details of aesthetics and how they function within individual panels on a minor scale. (This sort of analysis and understanding will be important as I compare panels and shots between comics and films in a direct fashion.) Yet *Understanding Comics* seems more interested in ideas such as how humans have been trained to read from left to right and top to bottom, why this has

[4] McCloud, Scott. *Understanding Comics: The Invisible Art*. New York, NY: HarperPerennial, 1994. Page 9.

occurred, and how this guides the norms of comic-book storytelling. This is interesting material that is certainly worth exploring, but ultimately it, and the book's focus on one aspect of comics that McCloud terms "closure," means it is slightly off the mark to becoming a focused aesthetic study.

McCloud describes "closure" as what the reader does in between panels or while they read a panel: they create the motion, time, and actions that one does not see but are suggested by the images. As McCloud puts it, "there lies a medium of communication and expression which uses closure like no other. A medium where the audience is a willing and conscious collaborator and closure is the agent of change, time and motion."[5] I believe McCloud is slightly in error in this assertion. Comics do not replicate the same subconscious closure that 24 frames per second bring, but I would argue that a cut in a film is very similar to a break in panels in a comic. The viewer or reader is asked to take the previous image and meld it to the current one, while they attempt to build the relationship between the two spaces presented. This is a difference of degree, not kind, between the two media. The real change is that there must be more breaks in a comic since motion or a moving panel is not possible. Closure seems to be one of the key points of McCloud's argument for what makes comics unique among media, and I simply don't agree with him enough to make this portion of his work a solid base for a study in aesthetics. Closure and what happens in between panels will of course be an aspect of this study, but it will not be a unifying force in the way that McCloud seems to assume it must be.

One of McCloud's other two books about comics, however, is a strong piece that has many useful applications for this study. *Making Comics* dwells on the inner workings of comics, and how panels, framing choices, and figure drawing all add to the art of storytelling in the world of comics. Where *Understanding Comics* goes broad, *Making Comics* achieves specificity. The book isn't perfect for this study and is primarily intended to help set artists on their way in the world of comics. Regardless, *Making Comics* still features a great deal of very interesting detail and enlightening specifics, such as noting how expressions in a comic may have to be exaggerated due to a lack of sound, making it hard to get across the unique inflection of dialogue that a film could handily convey.[6]

---

[5] Ibid, 65.

[6] McCloud, Scott. *Making Comics: Storytelling Secrets of Comics, Manga and Graphic Novels.* New York, NY: HarperCollins, 2006. Page 99.

Most of this book doesn't deal with how films and comics intersect, although McCloud doesn't shy away from noting how some film terminology is useful when making comics and mentioning that there are indeed connections between the two. He also doesn't avoid talking about prose and how the writing side of comics can sometimes employ novelistic techniques. McCloud has done some thinking about how comics and their capabilities intersect with other media; he just hasn't done much further writing on the subject.

Will Eisner and the Comics Form

Making Comics was another strong step along the way to establishing an aesthetic approach to comic analysis, but wasn't precisely what I needed. The final stop was actually recommended by McCloud himself. In his books there are constant references to Will Eisner and his works on comic-book storytelling. As such I read two books by Will Eisner: *Comics and Sequential Art*, as well as *Graphic Storytelling and Visual Narrative*. Both of these books were helpful and contain many useful, if sometimes narrow, points of view about how to "read" comics. This proceeds from Eisner's goal on these projects; the books are based on courses that Eisner taught on comic artwork, and they are intended as instructional pieces. This moves them away from presenting definitions and unifying theories of comics, like McCloud's *Understanding Comics*, and instead focuses them on showcasing how to craft comics that tell stories. Eisner goes into detail about how he created many of his own works and explains why he drew things in specific ways, dealing with topics such as backgrounds, panel layouts, the page as a whole, and how specific drawings affect the story. For instance, this is how Eisner describes the way certain panel sizes can affect the image contained within: "A narrow panel evokes the feeling of being hemmed in—confinement; whereas a wide panel suggests plenty of space in which to move—or escape. These are deep-seated primitive feelings and work when used properly."[7] This sort of explanation is a fantastic starting point for an analysis of comic-book aesthetics, but also highlights one of the weak points of Eisner's work. Sometimes he tends to simplify, as he does here, and almost states that any given device can only have one effect. A low angle in film is never guaranteed to mean the same thing regardless of context, but I doubt Eisner meant to imply that a narrow panel can only have one result for the

---

[7] Eisner, Will. *Comics and Sequential Art*. New York, NY: W. W. Norton & Company, 2008. Page 92.

reader. This flaw likely emerges from Eisner's instructional method. He is attempting to teach neophytes and so he tends toward simplifying concepts and working to craft a base level of understanding which will later be built into a more complex understanding of the medium through years of hard work.

Taking a closer look at the way in which Eisner pulls apart one of his own stories to explain how he fuses comic-book aesthetics with the story being told works well to highlight his general approach to the form and how he teaches it. He reprints a story featuring his famous character, the Spirit, which relies on a surprise, science-fiction-oriented ending. Eisner explains his approach to the story in this fashion: "In the following *Spirit* story, 'The Visitor' (13 Feb 1949), the requirements of stagecraft demand a firm, head-on perspective throughout. This is for the purpose of increasing the sense of reality in what would otherwise be a fantasy plot."[8] This basic level of understanding that seems too simple is what makes Eisner so important. He lends credence to all sorts of comic stories because he understands that any story will need form to support the content it contains. More importantly, Eisner understands that comics require their own visual language involving the manipulation of things such as panels, the style of art, the way characters are presented, and the way an entire page of panels presents an image to the reader's eye. Eisner was able to see all aspects of comics and had a lifetime of experience working with them, so his writings effortlessly explain the intricacies of the medium.

Moving forward through Eisner's description allows us to understand some basics of the medium and ways that we can consider it similar to or dissimilar from film. Many of the comments Eisner makes revolve around his decision to stress eye level depictions of events, allowing for realism to become the default tone of the story. Even when he breaks from this style he explains it as a way to further enhance realism: "Here is the sole instance in which a bird's eye view is undertaken. The intention is an orientation for a normal, everyday, believable setting."[9] Here we see something that could be easily replicated in film; eye level shots that stress realism and a lack of artistic presence can be used to set a viewer at ease and give a sense that everything is normal. Naturally, this would require other decisions to be made that comics do not have to deal with, such as what kind of camera movements would be used or if there would even be camera movements. It also presents different comic-book storytelling

---

[8] Ibid, 93.
[9] Ibid, 96.

techniques that must be kept in mind. Eisner explains other aspects of style that he deployed to stress the realism: "Every effort is made to keep the plot believable. The babies crawling all over the hero, the steady flat 'beat' of even ordinary (conventional) panels are all deliberately restrained."[10] Eisner's ultimate goal is teaching storytelling and these few examples of how he decided to tell a story show how naturally he is able to both create and then describe a story in a visual medium. This confirms an avenue of approach that McCloud laid out in his writing as well. What we see here is Eisner utilizing an aesthetically driven approach to analyze his comics, much in the same way that formalists approach analyzing films. His work is interested in how the language of comics can reinforce storytelling and most effectively influence readers. Since this book is mostly concerned with how films and comics shape their audiences' experiences, a formalist approach seems to be the most effective, and both McCloud and Eisner's well-regarded and effectively-written works confirm this kind of approach as a viable one.

Eisner also displays an interest in the differences between film and comics but doesn't end up spending too much time dealing with this issue. His ideas present some interesting basics, but never really gel into a cohesive or useful whole. For instance, Eisner describes ways in which comics and film differ by examining how their audiences interact with the two:

> The most important obstacle to surmount is the tendency of the reader's eye to wander. On any given page, for example, there is absolutely no way in which the artist can prevent the reading of the last panel before the first. The turning of the page does mechanically enforce some control, but hardly as absolutely as in film.[11]

Other small notes prove to be interesting, but the reasoning behind them starts to stray from Eisner's previously aesthetically-fueled analyses. Eisner draws a page of panels showing the difficulty that "cinematic" shots would present for a reader, and then follows this with another page where a more appropriate comic layout is presented to show the difference between the two types of storytelling. Eisner explains why readability breaks down, in his opinion, in the comic that utilizes filmic techniques: "The 'reading rhythm' of film rides on a flow of connected close-ups. This satisfies the 'movie-experienced' with understood action. The 'reading rhythm' of comics is slower because it involves

---

[10] Ibid, 96.
[11] Ibid, 40.

an intellectual input on a reader's real experience."[12] This is one instance when I'm not particularly convinced by Eisner's conclusion, especially considering the fact that it deals with social issues more than actual aesthetics. Eisner claims that movies use more close-ups because film viewers are trained to understand movies already. Eisner's approach here feels flawed; he speaks about film as a series of related close-ups that are legible due to a viewer's having seen a large number of films, which helps them understand film's unique language. This isn't completely wrong, but when Eisner then claims that comics do not function in this fashion something seems awry. Comics certainly speak their own language and have norms and traditions that help readers along. I'd like to move past the social approach (meaning the assumption that a medium can be defined by outside forces rather than its own internal construction) and apply formal ideas to each medium like Eisner does when he talks specifically about comics. It is likely that looking at general storytelling tendencies and basic preferences for specific kinds of stories (rather than trying to assign social reasoning to their aesthetic approaches) will illuminate the ways that the media diverge. So while Eisner ultimately understands comics, his comparison of comics to films leaves gaps that I hope this book will fill.

The Agenda of *Moving Panels*

After delving into these works on comics and their aesthetics, I am left with the belief that a formal methodology is the most useful way in which to approach this book. I intend to draw upon a school of thought known as Neoformalism. Neoformalism is a style of film analysis described by Kristin Thompson in her book *Breaking the Glass Armor: Neoformalist Film Analysis*. It is a reaction to work in the field of film studies that was largely predicated on psychoanalytic readings of texts that ultimately asked works to conform to a pre-determined methodology of understanding films and how they function. Formalism as an approach allows us to come to comics as a medium that interacts with its readers. Formalism stems from the fact that spectators of films are not merely observing, but participating. Films have the ability to provoke viewers to make assumptions, engage with the storyline, and to create what the film may not show. This is remarkably similar to McCloud's arguments about closure functioning uniquely in comics. A formalist approach also helps to

---

[12] Eisner, Will. *Graphic Storytelling and Visual Narrative*. Tamarac, FL: Poorhouse Press, 1996. Page 73.

correct the critic from an overreliance on more literary concepts, such as themes or symbolism, that currently dominate comics criticism. While talking about a book on Grant Morrison's comics, Kieron Gillen, a comic-book writer and former critic, effectively summed up his frustration with how comics criticism evades discussing aesthetic effects: "The avoidance of doing so fails to engage with comics as comics, rather than just as a vessel which carries ideas."[13] Both McCloud and Eisner deal with how to tell stories in the medium of comics. McCloud's work isn't primarily in this area though, and Eisner's work is more focused on crafting a full-fledged focus on aesthetics. In doing so Eisner (and McCloud somewhat in *Making Comics*) presents a formal analysis of his own comics as a way to teach aspiring comic artists.

Moving forward, I will be dealing primarily with how works of art have an effect on their audiences, how readers and viewers understand art, and the ways that they interact with both comics and films. Comparing these interactions helps us to understand the ways that the two media separate and converge. I will be moving away from the analysis of critics such as Douglas Wolk, and attempting to take on some of the issues that Scott McCloud brings up and push these issues further. Ultimately, both Scott McCloud and Will Eisner's works, while not exactly in line with my own thinking, will act as a guide for the style of comics analysis I will practice.

Now, it's important to address a few of the main issues that I hope to deal with and illuminate. There are three major topics that will help determine just what the differences between comics and films are.

First, how do the two media depict action? In this context, action can mean anything from a super-powered fistfight to a conversation. Do comics and films take similar approaches to these kinds of action or are there marked stylistic changes from the way that a film approaches a dialogue sequence in comparison to a comic-book? The pressures of word balloons in comics and the fact that dialogue must appear on the page would force different aesthetic choices on a comic storyteller than the concerns of filming the same dialogue sequence in a film. A director would have to deal with issues such as camera movement and how stylistic traditions (such as shot / reverse shot) can help the process of movie making function efficiently. We know that there will be unique

---

[13] Gillen, Kieron. *Scott Pilgrim Vs. the Universe*. 2009. gillen.cream.org/wordpress_html/?p=1689 (accessed 16 Mar 2009).

and different concerns that arise when making a movie and a comic, but by utilizing case studies we can begin to see exactly what those concerns may be.

Second, if comics are a purely visual medium while film is a medium that has both visual and aural elements, how does sound specifically influence either medium? Comics evoke sound through words and there can be no doubt that this will cause some level of disconnect in the aesthetic capabilities of the two media. Comics must evoke tone, timbre, and inflection in the visual depiction of the characters' dialogue. This means that words themselves are a stylized aspect of comics. Sound effects can blend into the artwork, titles can become physical parts of the comic's world, and dialogue balloons can be shaped and reshaped to evoke the way a character speaks. Conversely, films have the ability to do things such as suggest off-screen sound through the use of an original score and seamlessly incorporate music into the world of the story. Characters can speak for as long as they desire in a single shot without fear of dialogue overwhelming the image because words are not a physical aspect of the film. Simply put, sound, or the lack thereof in comics, is a clear demarcation that separates the two media. Examining how these shape the construction of a comic or film will be a key way to examine how the two media differ.

The final issue concerns the notion of time. Films move forward determined by the capture rate of digital or analogue film. A viewer sees one image and another follows and the two are stitched together creating a unified whole. This occurs 24 times a second, as one frame of film gives way to another and moves forward toward the film's conclusion. Viewers of a projected film cannot stop it, jump ahead, or reverse it. The film marches on and they are along for the ride. Comics also present a series of static images that must be unified into a whole, but instead of the seamless illusion of motion created by film, a comic places the images side by side on the page and asks a reader to use their mind to create what lies between the panels. In these panels, time stands still and it is up to the storyteller to help guide the reader through this experience, such as by breaking a single image into multiple panels to let the reader know that time is passing or by presenting a single character multiple times within the same panel to showcase their movement through a single space. Comics must constantly deal with the fact that their images cannot physically move on the page, so everything from which images are presented to how these frames are laid out in relation to one another must be directed toward helping animate the image in the reader's mind. Ultimately, I suspect that this issue will be one of the most important differences between the two media. Motion, camera movement, and a variety of other filmic tools can be approximated in comics through a variety of tricks, but a comic panel will never move and a storyteller must always be cognizant of this fact. This isn't necessarily a negative; it allows for a whole world of unique and divergent aesthetic capabilities that comics have access to. A montage of images arrayed on a page without any specific reading order is capable of evoking a specific mood which could never be recreated in an identical fashion through film, due to that medium's intrinsically linear nature. Examining the two media's unique relations to time will be a key aspect of this study.

Case studies that touch on one or more of these topics will help further illuminate these issues. I intend to compare the recent comic series *The Invincible Iron Man* with the first *Iron Man* film, and then look at both the comic and film versions of *Sin City*. These two adaptations will help us examine the depiction of action. The *Iron Man* material will point us toward the general tendencies of mainstream film and comics while the *Sin City* material will provide a film that attempted a more literal transition from comics to film. This will allow us to see what was changed and if unchanged moments are effective across the media. Next, I intend to move on to the film and comic versions of *Persepolis*. This case study will help illustrate all three topics and how a single creator can be strongly involved in the adaptation of their own work while still producing two vastly different results. I'll also be delving into both the film and comic versions of *Watchmen*. The film was one of the most ambitious adaptations of a comic undertaken in recent memory and is a fascinating look at how strict adaptations of material can rob a work of much of its original power and effectiveness. This case study will encapsulate all that we have learned up to that point and illustrate the strongest way to look at the concept of time in relation to comics and film. Lastly I'll be examining both Bryan Lee O'Malley and Edgar Wright's versions of *Scott Pilgrim*. O'Malley's *Scott Pilgrim* series is a transgressive, boundary-pushing work of comic art and storytelling, and Wright's film occupies a similar space within the world of cinema. They're two simpatico works that share a creative spirit even as they diverge in many important ways. This final work will bring together all the threads traced throughout the various chapters of this book.

A Quick Look at *Wanted*

To illustrate this point and to provide a primer for the kind of analysis I intend to undertake, I'd like to take a quick look at a few scenes from the comic and film versions of *Wanted*. These two works are both part of the mainstream of their respective media and fit comfortably into the world of action films and comics. Both pieces are successful in their construction and also work to illustrate how adaptations can alter their source's medium to most effectively adapt the story. *Wanted* is a particularly interesting case because the film version throws out almost all but the most basic elements of the comic's story. It moves from a story where super-villains take over the world to a story about a league of assassins who kill those who will ultimately cause problems for the world. Both stories still focus on the same basic character, Wesley Gibson, and his development into a killer, but the reasons for this are largely changed. The story was likely shifted because the comic deals with a large number of comic-book tropes that would have proven to be an unwelcome legal nightmare for a film (the comic features a variety of characters meant to evoke famous heroes such as Superman and Batman), though a few scenes still remain intact.

The scene I will examine takes place early in the story and is one of Wesley's earliest interactions with a group known as the Fraternity. Both versions of the scene feature the group forcing Wesley to shoot the wings off flies to help him understand his innate abilities as a killer. The first noticeable difference comes in the way that Wesley has a gun put to his head. In the comic, Professor Seltzer asks Fox to persuade Wesley in one panel and in the next panel we see Fox with a gun pointed at Wesley's head. The next panel features a close up of Wesley with Fox in the background still pointing the gun at him. This three panel sequence conveys the information in a way that is easily legible for a reader and helps to guide them through the beats of the story. The film also presents this situation, but handles the reveal of the gun pointed at Wesley's head in a much different fashion. In the film, Wesley tries to convince Sloan, the leader of the Fraternity, that he has him confused with someone else. This occurs in a straight on close-up of Wesley's face, while in the middle of a line of dialogue a "clunk" can be heard and Wesley tenses up while struggling through the end of his sentence. A slight camera move to the right follows this and reveals a man standing behind Wesley. He begins to speak and another cut occurs that showcases the gun pressed against Wesley's head. The film utilizes sound design and camera movement, two tools that are not

Wesley is forced to test his shooting acumen. From *Wanted* #1 (Dec 2003). Art by J. G. Jones.

available to comics, to surprise the viewer. The interruption of dialogue, as well as the sudden awareness of previously hidden space, redefines the action of the scene in a fashion that helps align the viewer with Wesley as well as increase tension. The comic does not surprise the reader and instead plays this portion of the scene in a slightly more humorous fashion, relying on the idiosyncratic Professor's dialogue to drive the moment along. This is a smart decision because a good comic creator knows that a reader's eyes will likely wander across a page, so retaining surprise in the reveal of the gun would need to be handled very carefully to succeed. It could be placed in the first panel of a page on the left side of the fold to create a surprise. This is because a large percentage of comics are presented two pages at a time, so any major reveals need to be kept for the left page. Otherwise, a viewer could easily glance to the second of the two pages at any moment and spoil a surprise. Taking this course would define the story's pacing in an extreme fashion, requiring the exact amount of story to allow this one moment to fall at one precise location. Ultimately, the reveal of a gun to Wesley's head doesn't deserve such attention. Writer Mark Millar, and artist J.G. Jones, de-emphasize the surprise of the moment and focus instead on the characters and their dialogue.

Also worth examining is the lead-up to Wesley shooting at the flies. Both the film and the comic emphasize this segment in different fashions. The film actually changes its story so it fits its aesthetic style. The film uses copious amounts of slow motion during its action sequences and this is explained as the characters having the ability to make their hearts beat faster than normal so as to release extra adrenaline into their bodies and thus slow down their perceptions of the world. This is accompanied by subjective shots that feature a warping view of the world and the pounding of a heart on the soundtrack. The construction of this scene relies heavily on this, focusing primarily on Wesley's face for his dialogue and then a subjective shot of the trashcan where the flies reside. This shot of the trashcan becomes progressively more distorted as Wesley's heart rate speeds up and similarly the soundtrack becomes louder and more focused on the beating of his heart as the tension mounts. This design is well-suited to film as it highlights Wesley's subjective experience through a distortion effect that is tied into movement and sound design reflecting Wesley's inner state.

The comic relies on different tools to help alert the reader to the rising tension and Wesley's experience. Color becomes a major component of the scene's design. The first three panels on the page consist primarily of green hues thanks to the Professor's bizarre experiments depicted in the background. When Fox begins to count to three, the background shifts; all of the elements that Jones previously drew disappear and the color changes from green to a mix of gray and red. The next panel carries this color scheme as well but in the third panel that depicts Fox pulling back the hammer of her gun, the entire background shifts to red while a yellow sound effect proclaims, "KLIK!" This strategy is particularly well-suited to comics because it is normal for the backgrounds of panels to be left vague due to the time constraints placed on artists who are putting out monthly issues. But I do not believe this is the reason why Jones stopped illustrating the background here. He is too meticulous in his construction to be that haphazard. It does explain, however, how easy it is to manipulate the background while remaining relatively subtle in a comic. If a film were to entirely obscure the background of a shot and replace it with a color it would be remarkably overt and that would undercut the tension. Once more, the two media alter similar base materials in order to most effectively represent them in different media.

This portion of the scene is worth considering further, because it is possible for film to eliminate background detail and replace it with color, but on film it would not be a particularly seamless device. It would transgress normal techniques of filmmaking and become distracting, while the use of such a device in comics is frequent and normalized. Ultimately the two media can differ even when they produce an image that is essentially the same. Of course, there are moments when the media converge. The comic and the film both focus intensely on Wesley's face at least once during this sequence. The film focuses on Wesley's face while he is shouting that he can't see the flies and the comic features a shot of the middle of Wesley's face when he expresses disbelief at what is occurring. Both film and comic focus on Wesley's experience through close-ups that help the reader see what Wesley is feeling. Another moment of convergence comes when Wesley fires his gun. While the film features a portion of these shots in slow motion, there is also a shot of Wesley firing rapidly at the flies that is nicely mirrored by a comic panel featuring a gun shooting a bullet with three spent casings hovering just above the weapon's chamber. Both depict essentially identical actions and do so in a way that is simply and readily replicated in a different medium. The relationship of the two media is a complex game of give and take, of similarity and difference. The

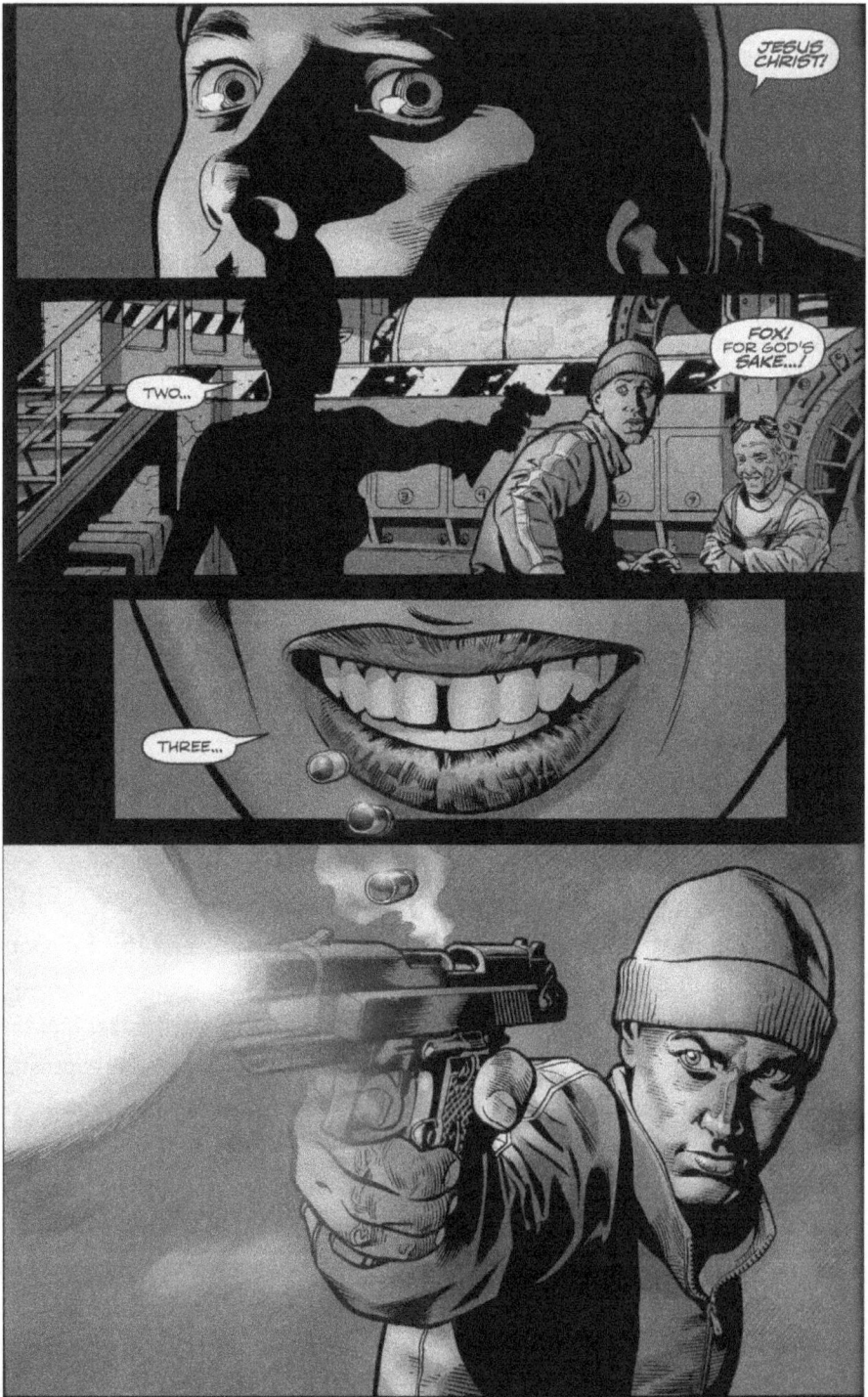

Continued from the previous page, a pressured Wesley fires his gun. From *Wanted* #1 (Dec 2003). Art by J. G. Jones.

adaptation of *Wanted* succeeds in achieving fidelity to the comic because it introduces new storytelling devices and story content that help replicate the effects of the comic in a different medium.

Conclusion

There are many different ways to approach particular scenes within a specific medium, and when adapting a work across media it becomes even more important that careful attention is paid to approach. This is vital in the conversion of comics to film where there are techniques that are not inherent to one medium. When one changes the medium of a story, the techniques' effect on the audience may change and the entire adaptation may crumble because of this. The ways in which film and comics will be forced to change their approaches to portray similar content is ultimately one of the most important aspects of this book. Discovering how often films and comics will coincide on the levels of content and form is key to understanding just how closely related the two media are, and will drive my analysis of both direct adaptations of source material like *Persepolis* and movies that primarily draw on characters as source material like *Iron Man*.

It is also worth keeping in mind how comic pages are constructed. As noted earlier, most pages will consist of multiple panels and will have another set of panels on the other side of the page. This is not the only possible construction, but it is the most prevalent, and will inform most of my discussions of panels since it is rare that they are entirely divorced from the page they are a part of. This does not mean that panels cannot be examined on their own, because it is important to look at the basic composition of a single panel and the information it depicts in the same way that it is important to look at a single shot in a movie and the way it depicts its portion of the story. But to truly understand a given shot, it is almost always necessary to look at what came before and what came after it, just as one must in a comic. This is an even more important aspect of analyzing comics than of film, since a comic page will be visible in its entirety at all moments. Page layout and the ways that panels interact is of importance to my analysis of comics and the ways that films can adapt them.

I hope this book will show just how different these films and comics can be and how the same stories can be represented in wildly different but equally successful fashions. The two media share certain tools and are both primarily visual, but there are distinct and clear differences that separate them. Comics and film may be closer than film and novels, but they are by no means identical. Drawing out and examining the unique capabilities of each medium is the primary goal of this book.

The Cinematic Comic

Comics are moving toward a "cinematic" style. This term has become a buzzword of late and I've yet to run into an actual definition of "cinematic" beyond the implication that it features realistic art and "widescreen" style panels. The trade paperback for *Wanted* features a blurb on the back cover that sums up the use of the word nicely: "With rollicking non-stop action, colorful characters and the sharpest dialogue around, *Wanted* comes as close to a cinematic comic as you're likely to find."[1] That quote doesn't really say anything; none of the traits listed clarify a definitive cinematic style. The movement toward cinematic comics speaks to how the glut of comic-book films have begun to influence their source material. More and more comics feature this style, even to the point where Marvel Comics' big summer event of 2006, *Civil War*, was drawn this way. As a case study, I will examine 2008's *Iron Man* alongside the first issue of the 2008 comic series *The Invincible Iron Man*, an ongoing series that was timed to coincide with the release of the film. This series was positioned to capitalize on the potential influx of new readers the film would ensnare. This does not imply that comics and cinema are naturally entwined because new readers become interested in comics after the films inspired by them are released. Rather, now comics attempt to capitalize on the aesthetics of film to sell themselves, showcasing the mutability and variety of aesthetic options available to comics. In doing so, the question then becomes whether or not it is possible for a comic to be truly cinematic, and if so, will it

---

[1] Millar, Mark and J.G. Jones. *Wanted*. Berkeley, CA: Top Cow, 2008. Back cover.

leave behind conventional comic storytelling techniques? *The Invincible Iron Man* departs from some traditional comic aesthetics to achieve a more cinematic look; it completely eschews typical sound cues and also organizes itself around widescreen panels for the majority of the book's pages. But does this aesthetic shift really make comics more like cinema? Ultimately the assumption of a "cinematic comic" is reductive. Replicating stories in a different medium requires care and an understanding of how each medium tells stories. Simply transcribing the visuals of a comic to film or vice-versa won't work because each medium is comprised of a unique set of tools and restrictions that dictate how stories can be told. Matt Fraction and Salvador Larroca, the writer and artist of *The Invincible Iron Man*, carefully structure their work to evoke cinema, but are careful not to neglect the conventions of comic-book storytelling while they do so. This helps them produce a unique aesthetic that resembles cinema in some ways, but is still a comprehensible comic in its own right.

The film and the comic were developed at the same time but were not directly tied to one another. Matt Fraction had little knowledge of the actual workings of the film even though he was tasked with creating a new-reader-friendly piece. He describes his thought process as such, "'I made a lot of guesses based on the film [that] I hoped the talent involved would make, and ended up being pretty simpatico.'"[2] Fraction did a remarkably good job of guessing at both the tone and character relations that the movie focused on. Both the film and the comic feature an almost identical cast. The major exception is the film's villain Obadiah Stane, who is replaced by his son in the comic (a new creation of the comic world), Ezekiel Stane. Similarly the characterization of Tony Stark strikes a middle ground between his playboy nature and his ultimate drive to make the world a better place. Of course, the actual stories diverge, but the feel of each piece is remarkably similar. The director of the film, Jon Favreau, also openly professed his appreciation for Fraction's work in the build up to *Iron Man 2*; "'I'll tell you which [comic books] we're looking at very closely, not so much for story but for tone: the Matt

---

[2] Marshall, Rick. "'Invincible Iron Man' Writer Matt Fraction Talks Comics / Movie Crossovers & Previews Issue #6." 2008. splashpage.mtv.com/2008/09/24/ invincible-iron-man-writer-matt-fraction- talks-comicsmovie-crossovers-previews-issue-6/ (accessed 3 Nov 2008).

Fraction [ones].'"[3] The interconnected nature of the works only grew from this point as Fraction was brought to Los Angeles to meet with Favreau and *Iron Man 2*'s co-writer Justin Theroux.[4] We can see that each work was influencing the other to some degree, but ultimately I will be focusing on the cinematic aesthetic that *The Invincible Iron Man* utilizes and how it compares to the aesthetic design of *Iron Man*, a solid representation of mainstream, big budget, comic-inspired filmmaking.

I'd like to start this comparison with the respective openings of both the film and the comic. For the film this means a Humvee ride in the Afghanistan desert as well as an attack on Stark's convoy. In the comic, the opening deals with a village in Tanzania and features some light exposition as well as a terrorist attack. Once more we can see parallels swiftly emerging between the works: both involve Third World violence in their spectacular openings, but these parallels are of less interest than the design choices that the film and the comic make. The film opens on a vista of the desert with some mountains in the background. This is handled with an extreme long shot and in the lower right hand side of the frame some movement is visible. The actual objects that are moving are hard to make out but dust is being kicked into the air and they are moving at a reasonable speed. The camera begins to pan to the left to follow the cars while wind blows on the soundtrack, the only audible noise. During this shot some studio credits are overlaid on the image, the only credits that will appear until the end of the film. This works well in the extreme long shot because the line of vehicles is not yet a strong visual, and so the eye is free to wander the frame. A cut in to the convoy soon occurs, placing the viewer just in front of the lead vehicle while a title appears that places the Humvees in "Kunar Province, Afghanistan." Accompanying this cut is a guitar riff as AC/DC's "Back in Black" begins to play. The noise of the vehicles themselves also join the soundtrack creating a stark contrast from the prior sound design that featured only the ambient wind noise. Here the film does an excellent job of crafting a

---

[3] Malone, Kevin. "*Iron Man* sequel will feature War Machine, Mandarin — and a dollop of Matt Fraction." 2008. blog.newsarama.com/2008/09/12/iron-man-sequel-will-feature-war-machine-mandarin-and-a-dollop-of-matt-fraction/ (accessed 11 Mar 2009).

[4] Marshall, Rick. "'Invincible Iron Man' Writer Matt Fraction Talks Comics / Movie Crossovers & Previews Issue #6." 2008. splashpage.mtv.com/2008/09/24/invincible-iron-man-writer-matt-fraction-talks-comicsmovie-crossovers-previews-issue-6/ (accessed 25 June 2012).

general tone for the opening scene using both shot scale and sound design. By utilizing a rather sedate first shot, Favreau emphasizes the cut to the more energetic second shot that features the Humvees driving straight at the camera. He mirrors this increase in energy in the soundtrack as well, adding rock and roll music along with the roar of the Humvees themselves. Matthew Libatique's editing reinforces this contrast, utilizing a somber, prolonged first shot and then accelerating the pace of the editing as the scene shifts into the lighter tone of the Humvee ride. This quick change in tone and pace also highlights the fact that the viewer isn't in a restrained drama but a rollicking action film, instantly setting the stage for all that is to follow. Though these are just the first few moments of the opening scene of the film, they work well as a comparison to the first page of the comic.

The comic opens similarly, with an extreme long shot. This shot is at ground level, though, and places the reader in the center of a town that is denoted as "Tabora, Tanzania. Africa." by the title on the panel. This establishing shot is smaller in scale than the film's, but, interestingly, features no visual center. It consists of a large number of pedestrians and houses but has no focal point. This seems tied in to the story's need to establish the village as a populated place that will soon be decimated by terrorists. The problem then arises that it is difficult to focus a reader in on a specific character in such a populated panel. A film could use motion or camera movement to bring out an important character, like the vehicles driving across the desert in the film. Comics do not have the luxury of these tools, and so this establishing shot forgoes centering the characters that will carry this scene and instead focuses on Tony Stark's narration and the general idea of a populated village. It is also important to note that, in the comic, this panel helps to establish the dominant panel type for the entire issue, which emphasizes a horizontally oriented, rectangular view of the story, similar to widescreen compositions in film. This panel is larger than any of the others on this page in terms of height but it is still wider than it is tall and conforms to the "widescreen" aesthetic that is being established. The two establishing shots do a good job of constructing the basis for what is to come. The film sets an atmosphere that is quickly undercut to heighten the enjoyment of the raucous and humorous scene that immediately follows while the comic details important information that will help the reader comprehend the events that will follow.

Matt Fraction begins his Iron Man run. From *Invincible Iron Man* #1 (July 2008). Art by Salvador Larroca. Copyright © Marvel Comics.

The compositions themselves do not seem particularly linked to either medium, but the ultimate design does feel subtly different. The film highlights the motion of the Humvees through the desert in the opening shot, drawing the eye to them both through the dust the cars kick up and also through the barren nature of the frame itself. The comic fills its frame but knows it will be difficult to draw the reader's eye through such a densely populated panel and thus decides to leave it blank rather than squeeze important characters into frame since they might be missed. The two establishing shots could be replicated in either medium, but the exact way they are handled here feels suited to the media in which they are represented. The film highlights motion and sound design to further emphasize a tonal shift that is coming while the comic focuses on conveying information in a clear fashion that will not confuse readers. This is important for any single issue of a comic because it is so much shorter in length than a film and clearly establishing a location and characters is essential to maximizing the story contained in the 22 pages provided. This speaks to how similar shots can be subtly tweaked to be more effective in one medium or another. These shots are more effectively keyed in to the needs and pressures of their respective media, rather than acting as functional equivalents.

From this point onward, both the comic and the film continue to establish their dominant tones. The film features a comedic sequence where Tony Stark jokes around with the occupants of his Humvee. Dialogue largely carries this sequence forward so it isn't particularly necessary to delve into it on an aesthetic level but it does have one important feature worth noting. There are plenty of reaction shots that feature all three of the occupants of the vehicle who are not Tony Stark. This becomes important because this scene's jocular tone will soon be undercut by a vicious assault that will feature the death of all three escorts. Favreau wants to establish a link between the viewer and these minor characters and he does this through both the humorous dialogue and a visual connection to the characters. Thus, when we see them die we have characters that may not have names but do have distinct faces and personalities, and so we are more likely to care about their deaths. By finding out more about these characters and understanding their human qualities, the viewer is connected to the characters, so when they are killed it quickly establishes a moral divide between good and bad that involves the viewer on an emotional level. Individually, these reaction shots would not be difficult to replicate in a comic, but the sheer number of them is worth noting. There are a total of thirty-six shots in one minute and twenty-three seconds of screen time for an average shot length of 2.31 seconds. This is fairly fast for a simple dialogue scene, and the rest of the other dialogue scenes I clocked in this film came in at over three seconds per shot. Part of this disparity can be explained away by the fact that the scene is shot inside a Humvee, but the scene itself suggests this is not the only reason for the speedy cutting. Favreau hits multiple reaction shots and even keeps the camera on the soldiers while Stark is talking off-screen, suggesting the importance of seeing these characters' faces. So while the cutting is likely influenced by the film's need to shoot within a car it also seems that the speed of the editing is a result of giving all of the soldiers as much face time as possible.

In comparing the media, the issue then becomes whether or not a single panel holds the same level of importance as multiple shots in a movie. The sheer repetition of the soldiers' faces holds a stronger place in the viewer's mind than a single panel in a comic could manage. This doesn't mean that a comic would be unable to evoke empathy for characters that are only ancillary to the story. It might be harder to do so in the presence of main characters who get the most face time in the limited space that a mainstream comic-book provides. The introduction of *The Invincible Iron Man* seems to support this claim because it features an ancillary character that the audience is asked to care for and does so by focusing on her visually while Tony Stark remains off frame, narrating in captions on the page.

After the establishing panel, the comic moves to a second panel that shifts toward the focus of this page: three girls who have just purchased a cell phone. The most important of these three is Adimu, who is dressed in bright green with a red bandanna. This outfit quickly holds the reader's attention even though she is flanked by her two friends, thanks to their softer shades of purple that do not catch the eye as effectively. Stark's narrative captions help to establish Adimu's world, as well as the impact that a cell phone will have on her young life. The next panel shifts behind the girls to highlight the cell phone itself. A high angle shot is used and, since the characters' backs are presented to the reader, the focus is primarily on the cell phone, which helps to highlight the technological theme of this issue. Consequently, the comic will tread the same path as the film by presenting a terrorist attack that will kill these minor characters. In *Iron Man* this results in a scene with quicker than usual editing for a dialogue sequence, while in *The Invincible Iron Man* it results in an opening that features only the narration of the main character rather than his physical appearance. Both succeed in making the reader empathize with the characters but do so in subtly different ways. The film maximizes the appearance of these characters even though the main character is present, but the comic decides to excise the main character from the scene on a visual level because featuring both Stark and the minor characters would eat up valuable space.

The differences presented in these sequences are interesting in that each medium is attempting the same thing: stirring empathy for characters who do not have much of a presence in the story. Also of note is the fact that each accomplishes this in roughly the same fashion: by giving said characters more face time. The important distinction, however, is that this manifests in slightly different ways. Both deemphasize Tony Stark, but the film is still able to retain his presence within the scene through tools such as off-screen sound and rapid editing. The comic instead completely excises Tony Stark's visual appearance, instead focusing on his off-panel voice, characterized by the yellow text boxes with red outlines. These colors bring to mind the Iron Man armor since the majority of readers would know what Iron Man looks like prior to starting the issue, either through prior experience or simply by looking at the cover of the comic. This is essentially a functional equivalent for the sound of a character's voice. By color-coding narration panels, a reader can quickly associate characters with certain words, even when they are not visually linked to the panels in any other way. In the end, we see two scenes that strive to balance their main characters with ancillary characters, but utilize a different set of tools to retain this balance – once more highlighting how films and comics are able to accomplish similar tasks with differing techniques.

Now that the minor characters have been established, it will be useful to move on to the moment in both the comic and the film when the scenes shift tonally. Both accomplish this deftly, but do so in ways that feel remarkably well-suited to their media. The film features a shot of a soldier preparing to take a picture of another soldier with Tony Stark. The soldier taking the picture is in the front seat of the Humvee, so while the viewer watches him with the camera they are able to see the next Humvee further up the road. The shot is established before cutting back to Tony and the soldier, and then returns for a moment before the Humvee further up the road explodes. The film creates a stasis of sorts with the initial shot. The viewer sees the Humvee ahead and the soldier fiddling with the camera, and all seems fine. We cut away from that shot and watch the other soldier try to instruct the first one in the use of the camera before cutting back. When the film cuts back to the soldier in the front seat, the viewer expects more of the playful banter and lighthearted tone that has been delivered so far in the scene. This expectation is quickly undermined by a violent explosion further up the road. This explosion in the background of the shot destroys the stasis that had previously been established in the shot / reverse shot pattern. To further hammer this point home, the music on the soundtrack cuts out, distancing the viewer from the previously comedic tone even further. Favreau wants to emphasize the abrupt and frightening nature of the attack and does so by creating a scene that starts as a comedy but quickly shifts gears. He does this by establishing both a visual and aural world that is clearly defined and then redefined by the assault. He relies on the tools at his disposal to put the viewer in a specific frame of mind and then uses those same tools once more to surprise the viewer and signal the new tone that is taking over the scene.

The comic is also able to highlight such a shift in tone, and the end of the first page features just such a shift. The first page structures itself around Tony Stark talking about Adimu buying a cell phone with her friends and how cell phones are easier for many people in Third World nations to own than a landline. This establishes an informative tone since the reader is learning about these characters and their world. Afterwards, the impromptu lesson gives way to a more personal one as the page progresses and by the final panel the narration even features a joke, echoing the comic foundation of the film's opening scene. In the end, though, the page takes a tragic turn as Tony Stark laments Adimu's death in a narration box overlaid on the final panel. To highlight this emotional moment the comic utilizes a strategy that film would be hard pressed to recreate. The final panel on the page breaks the established panel size by overlaying an almost square close up of Adimu over another panel that would have conformed to the rest of the "widescreen" compositions. The tonal and emotional shift that occurs between these two panels is highlighted by the juxtaposition of one panel over the other. The narrative shift, and the panel in which this shift occurs, literally breaks the established aesthetic of the page's layout to help highlight the change. Again we see an important change in the tone of a story being marked stylistically through interrupting the established method of storytelling. The film does so through depth staging, sound design, and moment-to-moment development of shots: three techniques that are well-suited to a medium that has the ability to showcase actual movement and sound. The comic, on the other hand, utilizes the fact that its "shots" co-exist on the same page and establishes a traditional type of panel that will then be interrupted when the tone of the story is interrupted. This once more highlights how each medium has a rhythm that can be both established and interrupted in unique ways, further showcasing just how difficult it can be to achieve fidelity in an adaptation if a creator decides to merely copy compositions rather than to adapt the material in a way that translates the overall effect to a different medium.

Now that we've examined the two openings and the ways that they utilize divergent approaches to similar material, I'd like to focus on something that would seem a tad simpler: dialogue. Both film and comics present a unique challenge in this arena. For film, breaking down into shot / reverse shot patterns is usually the norm for dialogue scenes, but it isn't, in general, a particularly dynamic shooting style either.

Favreau does attempt to avoid shot / reverse shot construction at times through staging and character movement but ultimately most of the dialogue scenes adhere to this pattern. For instance, a scene that features Tony Stark and Obadiah Stane talking starts with Tony climbing to the top of a flight of stairs to enter a room. He then crosses to the right of the frame and sits down on a couch near Pepper Potts while some close-up shots of Obadiah playing the piano are inserted to both build the space and move in more closely on Jeff Bridges, the actor playing Obadiah Stane. This then leads to a long shot where Obadiah stands up while talking, walks down to Tony's location, and sits down next to him. This places Obadiah on the left of the frame, Tony in the middle, and Pepper on the right. This shot lasts 15 seconds but it quickly gives way to a shot / reverse shot setup consisting of a medium close-up of Obadiah over Tony's shoulder and another medium close-up of Tony over Obadiah's shoulder. This will be broken by a line of dialogue from Pepper during her own medium close-up, divorced from the shot / reverse shot pattern. This then causes a cut to a shot that focuses on Obadiah. In this shot, Tony turns his head around to look at Pepper, repurposing his portion of the shot / reverse shot to connect the new space that has entered into the dialogue. Obadiah takes back the dialogue though, and Tony turns to him once more, re-establishing the prior shot / reverse shot pattern. The shot / reverse shot breaks down as Tony begins to leave the room in a tracking shot, but Obadiah re-engages him in a conversation, setting up a new shot / reverse shot pattern which is then broken as Tony leaves the room for good.

Overall, what we can see here is Favreau making the most of small portions of a dialogue scene that break the shot / reverse shot pattern in an effort to keep the film interesting while also working to support the dramatic development of the scene. On the other hand, the film still falls back into the shot / reverse shot setup every so often because it is a quick and effective way to shoot a dialogue scene. What this scene effectively demonstrates are the concerns that Favreau handled as a filmmaker and the pressures that the medium of film exerted on him. He could have very easily fallen into a simple shot / reverse shot pattern that was never broken or tried for a long unbroken take of the entire scene but each would have presented problems. More shot / reverse shot would simply be a boring choice visually and would also be less effective in marking turning points within the scene. Longer takes would have created difficulties in staging and setup that breaking down into shot / reverse shot helps avoid, not to mention the help that shot / reverse shot provides in post-production and the editing room. Favreau strikes a middle ground that both relies on shot / reverse shot patterns but violates them at times. And it is this understanding of filmmaking norms and practices that helps this scene function effectively.

A dialogue scene in *The Invincible Iron Man* presents a whole different array of challenges for the creators, and these differing challenges speak to the disparities of the two media. In dialogue heavy scenes, the established aesthetic of "widescreen" panels begins to break down in favor of a larger number of square panels arranged to space out the dialogue so as not to overwhelm any one image with a clutter of text. This speaks to a concern that is unique to comics. In film, dialogue can exist unobtrusively within a shot as it is merely sound, but since comics must represent noise visually, sound takes up physical space in panels. Because of this, too much "sound" in any one panel will cause a loss of visual legibility. This in turn forces the writer and artist to think of ways to retain legibility while adhering to the style of storytelling necessary. I would not argue that the first issue of *The Invincible Iron Man* is entirely successful in this regard since the "widescreen" aesthetic does disappear when dialogue takes precedence, but the comic retains the look that it has established for the most part.

A conversation from *Invincible Iron Man* #1 (July 2008). Art by Salvador Larroca. Copyright © Marvel Comics.

The same conversation continues. From *Invincible Iron Man* #1 (July 2008). Art by Salvador Larroca. Copyright © Marvel Comics.

These two pages from the first issue summarize the contrasts in *The Invincible Iron Man*'s visual design. The second page features five widescreen panels. The first page features six panels and is decidedly different in appearance than the second page. Why does this occur and could it have been avoided? The answer lies in the action that is being depicted. The first page features three shots of Ezekiel by himself while he talks to people in a boardroom. This can be readily compared to the second page that features only one shot of Ezekiel on his own. The single shot of Ezekiel is, frankly, rather boring. Ezekiel stands before a monotonous gray background and points at himself while a shadow can be seen at the bottom left of the panel. If the first page were to construct itself around widescreen panels there would be a minimum of three full panels of this kind and the page would be dull to look at. To combat this, the panels instead become squared and more focused on his face while allowing the word balloons to cover up the majority of the dull gray in the background.

There were ways to retain the widescreen aesthetic of panels on this page, but it is worth noting why they were not used. The same information on the first page could be conveyed by merging the last two panels into one widescreen composition and then placing the two sets of word balloons on both side of Ezekiel's head to cover up most of the gray. This solution would lead to a remarkably wordy panel, weighted too heavily toward text, rather than using the combination of words and images that is so important to comics. In an effort to keep the page visually stimulating, it is broken down into more panels that do not individually conform to the widescreen aesthetic. When one looks at the page as a whole, a different image begins to emerge. It is possible to view the six panels as three widescreen strips on the page; the first panel conforming on its own, the next three creating the second strip, and the last two establishing a final strip along the page. This construction of like-sized panels fashioned uniformly gives an impression of a widescreen design. Aiding this impression is the small amount of blank white space that is left between each panel. When the page is viewed as a whole, this minimizes the break between panels, and leads the reader to think of the panels as widescreen strips more readily. Also worth noting is the fact that each strip features a unique number and size of panels that remains constant. This creates a unity for each widescreen layout that helps differentiate them at a glance when one views the page as a whole. So ultimately, while the widescreen aesthetic is broken down on a base level, fragmentary portions remain.

This page is one of the most successful in the issue but there are dialogue pages that do not succeed in the same way. In one instance, the page breaks down into a two by four grid of identical square panels and it is hard to say that it replicates the widescreen aesthetic of the rest of the issue. These design choices all speak to the concerns that the comic's creators faced when scripting and drawing a dialogue scene. It is nevertheless apparent how far divorced the analysis of the film's dialogue sequence is from the analysis of the comic's. Both grapple with radically different problems and must deal with spatial and visual constraints. It is fascinating that, when a comic attempts to replicate cinematic aesthetics, it encounters problems pertaining to comics rather than cinema. Once more we see that the cinematic comic is primarily cinematic for the reader, but not for the creators.

The film utilizes shot / reverse shot setups to help guide and structure the scene but breaks from them to comment on turning points and to present a varied image that will keep a viewer from becoming bored by repetitive visuals. The comic structures its panel choices and layouts around similar concerns, dealing with how the dialogue will lay out on the page and then how this dialogue will contribute to the visual design as well as whether it will bore or excite the reader. Fraction and Larroca strike a similar balance to Favreau in that they vacillate between the traditional aesthetic they have established and breaking this aesthetic to present a more exciting image. The storytelling reflects this, allowing for two dialogue scenes that effectively get across the information intended while varying the visual presentation in two strikingly different fashions. We see the film dealing primarily with issues such as shot length and the kinds of shots to be utilized while the comic deals with how to parcel out the dialogue while also considering how to frame the panels as a complete unit on the page.

Still, there remains one important component of the two works to discuss: the action scene. These sorts of scenes are extremely important to both mainstream comics and films, and no evaluation of cinematic comics would be complete without some examination of how an action scene is handled. I'll be taking a look at two action scenes involving Iron Man himself: (1) the film scene depicting Iron Man striking back at Raza and his terrorist group and (2) Iron Man's raid on A.G.M. (Advanced Genocide Mechanics) in the comic.

Both of the scenes begin with Iron Man flying down into the action. The film starts by showing Iron Man rocket to the ground through a subjective shot. Though the camera is placed in a location where a terrorist or civilian might reside, this potential character is never visualized. The point-of-view evokes the feeling of "being in" the action. This is very similar to panels 1, 4, and 5 of the two pages shown below. Iron Man reaches his destination, hovers above the ground for a short period of time and then lands on the ground in a crouching position (although the comic adds a punch to the landing). The subjective location of the "camera" is utilized here in the fourth panel of the first page. This causes some problems for the comic's cinematic aesthetic though. The action of hovering above the enemies can only be effectively represented with a vertical panel and this causes a breakdown in the widescreen aesthetic. Three of the four panels on this page could have easily worked as "widescreen" panels but the content of the final panel cannot be presented horizontally. This consideration then shapes panels two and three into a vertical configuration that does not abide by the widescreen styled compositions we are used to from this issue. The first panel of the page still uses this widescreen setup but none of the other panels can be massaged into this design while the content of the panels remain as is.

Another interesting trait of this layout is that vertical reading takes precedence over right to left reading due to the final image of Iron Man descending. To help emphasize this reading pattern, a portion of the narration is placed between two panels so that the reader will follow the action down instead of the traditional reading flow of left-to-right. One could argue that film has its own conventions to grapple with, such as the 180-degree rule (a.k.a. the axis of action).[5] While this is true, I would argue that the comics are also concerned with many of these same issues. Legibility of story and choice of image affect a comic in a similar way to a film, but comics must also wrestle with how the images will look when a reader can simply glance from one to another at any point they desire. Because of this, page layouts become a concern that is unique to comics and must be dealt with while constructing a scene.

---

[5] This rule, which in theory confines the camera to 180 degrees around a subject (such as two characters talking), helps prevent viewer confusion, essentially by keeping what's on the left on the left and what's on the right on the right, despite cutting to different shots and camera angles.

An action scene from *Invincible Iron Man* #1 (July 2008). Art by Salvador Larroca. Copyright © Marvel Comics.

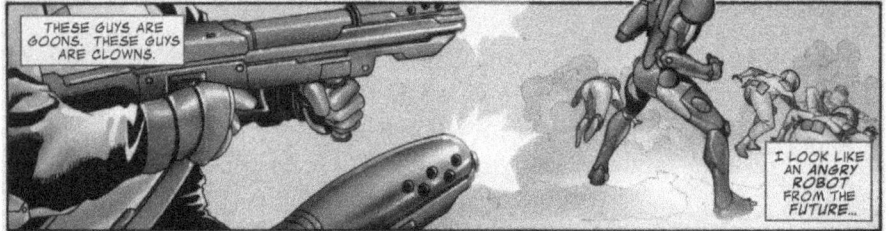

The same action scene continues. From *Invincible Iron Man* #1 (July 2008). Art by Salvador Larroca. Copyright © Marvel Comics.

One technique that we see utilized in the film's action sequence that we do not see in the comic is a certain kind of editing, the "match on action" (in which an action continues from one cut to the next, helping to blend the two shots). After Iron Man lands in the film, he punches one foe and then turns to shoot another who is off-screen. When the beam is fired, a cut occurs and we see the beam striking the soldier. Iron Man then swings just slightly to the right toward another foe and the camera re-centers on this enemy. He charges up a beam and fires, and just as the beam slams into the enemy, Favreau cuts to a new angle that shows the enemy being thrown back. This is a "match on action" and feels like a filmic technique that a comic would find very difficult to replicate. The cut reinforces the impact of the beam by jarring the viewer ever so slightly at the exact moment that the blast would land. The cut doesn't violate the 180-degree rule or any other editing constraint, but it does break an action that mirrors the effect of the blast itself. Attempting to split an action such as this between two panels would be odd to say the least. Two differing angles of the same beam blast would likely be read as Iron Man firing off two separate shots, since comics deal in static images and readers understand that they are being asked to fill in the blanks between panels. Instead, the comic features panels where Iron Man shoots a beam from each hand into a large crowd of bad guys or a panel where he releases bombs from the armor in the direction of the viewer. These panels do a solid job of presenting clear images that require only a small amount of reader input. This helps create a concise and easily understandable action sequence that then allows the reader to focus on the excitement of the action rather than trying to decipher what is occurring in the first place. It also maximizes the amount of action that can be presented. If the story were to dwell on what happened before and after each and every punch, it would eat up valuable page space. Fraction and Larroca boil the sequence down to its essentials and do not include a formal technique like the "match on action."

We've mentioned how excitement is generated in the first place with the film's use of editing to reinforce action, but it will be useful to look at a few shots and panels to pull out some other ways that the film and the comic attempt to create dynamic images that will involve their audiences. One way that both the film and the comic do this is by focusing the action toward the viewer. In the film, this means that when Iron Man flies, it is almost always directly at the viewer. Iron Man flies down toward the ground, and the camera tilts down with him. When he takes off to the next location, he flies in a graceful arc but ends up facing the camera and moving quickly in the direction of the viewer. Similarly, many of his beams are shot toward the viewer. The comic also likes to use this kind of "forward" movement. One panel features Iron Man speeding away from an explosion in the background of a panel and directly toward the reader (this is mirrored in the film when Iron Man blows up a tank and walks toward the viewer as it blows up in the background); another shows Iron Man shooting bombs toward the reader. There are seven panels that showcase Iron Man on these two pages and five of them have Iron Man moving toward or facing the reader. While the effectiveness of confronting the viewer with the action is a subjective matter, it is a tactic uniformly adopted by both comics and film particularly in regard to action sequences.

Once more we see that while there are certain areas in which comics and films collide, there are also areas that remain separate. Whether it is a dialogue scene, the opening of a story, or an all-out action sequence, comics and films are constantly grappling with pressures from their respective media's storytelling norms, and from the content of their stories. All of these issues shape the ways that the stories are being told. In comparing *Iron Man* and *The Invincible Iron Man*, the most basic aesthetic concerns shape the two pieces. For the comic, the existence of panels upon a page structures a majority of the layouts and how the story is told. The film instead focuses on tools such as editing and motion to communicate its message. While Fraction and Larroca must deal with the overt juxtaposition of images on a page, Favreau pays attention to the fact that film can sharply contrast moments through tools such as editing and sound design because of the strictly linear nature of the medium. These two works form the basis for a particularly useful set of comparisons because they present a film and a comic that are both aspiring toward cinematic storytelling. While that isn't particularly surprising for the film, it does raise quite a few questions about the comic. It seems that while the comic does manage to replicate an aesthetic that is reminiscent of cinema, it does so in a way that operates from a working knowledge of comic techniques and devices. This understanding of comics and the willingness to mold them into a cinematic shape results in a work that appears superficially as "cinematic" but is still a comic in terms of its core aesthetics. Even when the two media converge, they are still very different vehicles for storytelling.

Sinful Motion

The Invincible Iron Man comics and the 2008 *Iron Man* film helped illuminate some of the ways that comics and film tell stories within their two respective media. The comparison also helped explain how comics could be "cinematic" in ways that didn't necessarily have anything to do with the basics of filmic storytelling. However, while both examples employed a similar character and tone, neither was directly related to the other in terms of content. It is therefore useful to take a closer look at a film adaptation of a comic that attempts to accurately replicate its source material. Doing so will further our understanding of how these two media are related.

Robert Rodriguez and Frank Miller's adaptation of *Sin City* (Miller's iconic gritty, noir comic) is one such adaptation. Rodriguez was so enamored with the property and Miller's vision for it that he ended up having to quit the Director's Guild of America so he could bring Miller on as co-director of the project.[1] Rodriguez wanted Miller's comic-book vision to be brought to the screen and he was unwilling to move forward with the project without Miller's co-directing. This makes the film and comics an ideal case study since the original creative voice was included with the adaptation. Therefore, there can be no doubt that the two works are intended to emulate one another in style and substance.

---

[1] "Rodriguez Quit DGA to Make *Sin City*." 30 May 2005.
contactmusic.com/new/xmlfeed.nsf/story/rodriguez-quit-dga-to-make-sin-city
(accessed 11 Feb 2011).

The intention of the film's creators and their desire to construct a work of art that is reverent to the original are clear. In a special feature on the DVD, Rodriguez states his intentions for the film quite simply: "I started really looking at it as instead of trying to turn it into a movie, which would be terrible, let's take cinema and try and make it into this book."[2] To that effect, Rodriguez and Miller ended up relying heavily on green screen techniques to give the film a stylized look that largely attempts to remain as faithful to the comic as possible. But how did Rodriguez and Miller set about this feat of turning a movie into something akin to a comic? Did their attempt to do so wind up being an artistic success or a well-intentioned mistake? The best way to determine just how Rodriguez and Miller re-envisioned cinema as a comic with their adaptation is to look at a few scenes from the film.

One scene featured in both the movie and the first *Sin City* collection (originally titled *Sin City* and since retitled *Sin City: The Hard Goodbye*) explores this concept dutifully. In it, Marv (the protagonist) realizes that a woman, Goldie, whom he slept with the night before, was murdered while the pair slept and that he is about to be framed for the crime. This comic sequence begins with a large splash page from an overhead vantage point as police storm up the stairs toward Marv and Goldie's rented room. The comic then moves to a regimented two-by-three grid of panels showcasing Marv's preparation for the oncoming brawl. The film uses the same basic layout and sequence of events but with a few minor, yet not inconsequential, changes. First, while Marv readies for the fight, the film cuts back out to the hallway and adds a shot of the officers moving toward the room. The reason this was done was likely to keep the viewer tense; it's a short sequence and the audience is unlikely to forget that the police are on their way. The subtle flashes of red across the screen during the tender moment where Marv holds Goldie's lifeless hand remind the viewers of the encroaching law enforcement and their idling squad cars outside, but a cut to their forward motion hammers home this point more effectively and viscerally. The comic doesn't feel this is necessary; it's content with the single, full-page image and then six panels of just Marv. Four of these panels feature Marv taking some pills. One has the policemen's voices overlaid on Marv's fist while commanding him to open the door, and the final is a close up of Marv's face as he promises to be right out. Why the comic doesn't feature a

---

[2] Rodriguez, Robert. "Behind the Scenes." *Sin City*. DVD. 2005.

Police storm up the stairs. From *Sin City: The Hard Goodbye*. Art by Frank Miller. Copyright © Frank Miller, Inc.

panel of the police moving toward Marv's room is clear when one observes both pages in tandem. The splash page of the cops charging up the stairs is on the left side of the fold, while the two by three grid is on the right side of the fold. This means that while the reader is watching Marv prepare, they can still see the police charging up the stairs out of the corner of their eye. There's no need to inject a panel of police in that grid because they haven't left the viewer's eyesight, and they never will completely. Since comic panels don't exist in a vacuum, there's no chance of a reader blocking the cops from their field of vision, unlike a film wherein once an image has left the screen, it is wholly removed for good unless a director wants to return to it in a future shot. The co-existence of images on a page makes the tension palpable without the need to return to the image within the forward progress of the story. In the film, however, a shot is injected into the sequence to help keep the tension high and remind the viewer of the approaching danger. It's a change designed to better serve the demands of a different medium and a good indicator that while Rodriguez and Miller intend to stick closely to the source material, they aren't interested in wholly replicating it at every turn.

Once Marv decides to leave his room, there is another moment where the film deviates ever so slightly from the comic. Both the comic and the film cut from inside of Marv's room, where he tells the police he'll be right out, to the outside, as Marv crashes through his door, shattering the wood and knocking multiple officers off their feet. Both accentuate this explosion of action but they do so in different ways. The comic utilizes a panel that fills roughly two-thirds of the page, whereas the previous page featured six panels in a regimented two by three grid. Changing the pattern of the storytelling makes the moment hit harder. Miller also places it as the first panel on a left page so a reader doesn't see it coming until they turn the page. This allows Miller to retain the moment's sudden, abrupt acceleration, since it is unlikely that a reader will have accidentally glanced at the next page prematurely. This sort of problem isn't something a film has to worry about. On the other hand, it's not quite possible for a film to make the screen bigger without doing something drastic like changing the movie's aspect ratio to create a different image size. Instead, the film uses two uniquely film-based techniques to create a similar experience for the viewer. The first technique aims to replicate the slow, steady pattern of the two by three grid of the comic. The film does this by lingering on Marv's face for roughly five seconds as the cops bang on the door and Marv replies to their

Marv explodes onto the police. From *Sin City: The Hard Goodbye*. Art by Frank Miller. Copyright © Frank Miller, Inc.

request to open it. While five seconds isn't a substantial amount of time, the image is essentially static. After Marv finishes his dialogue, the shot still remains for just a moment. Something is about to happen and the viewer knows it, but they are held with Marv just before the violence erupts. When the film does end up cutting to the shot of Marv destroying the door, the second technique kicks in: the jump cut. As the camera cuts outside of the room, Marv immediately breaks through the door; a split second after the door has splintered, the film rapidly cuts to a new angle that is just barely different than the first. This is a violation of traditional continuity editing and by making this choice Rodriguez and Miller are accentuating the sudden burst of energy that has occurred in the film. This is a technique that can't be replicated in comics, or at least not as the film portrays. Comics can repeat panels, but it's rare to see two panels back to back that have a slight change in perspective. Repeated panels usually slow down a scene by emphasizing a particular moment or showcasing a still character for an extended period of time. Therefore, these kinds of techniques are usually deployed in slower, less action-packed sequences. In a film, where time always advances, a quick cut to another near identical angle jars the viewer and highlights the action that is taking place. Such a cut would be ill suited for a calmer sequence, but here the rapid shift in speed that occurs in the scene is perfectly paired with a swift, jagged approach to editing, a technique that Rodriguez and Miller will utilize more than once to accentuate moments such as these.

After Marv has escaped from the police by commandeering a squad car, he drives it off a dock and into the water. He extricates himself from the car and, as he swims away from it, narrates his intentions toward the people who killed Goldie. The comic depicts Marv swimming in two panels; the first is a long shot with Marv in the foreground of the image and the sinking car in the background of the image. The second is a close-up of Marv's gruesome, resolved expression. The film handles this sequence in an identical fashion with the first shot featuring Marv swimming in a long shot while the car sinks in the background and the second shot featuring a close-up of Marv's face. Oddly though, the transition in the film version of this sequence feels different than in the comic. Since a comic is composed of specific images deployed to tell a larger story, the abrupt change from long shot to close-up isn't all that surprising a choice because a reader can be expected to fill in the blanks between the two moments. In a film, though, it's a large change to make so quickly, especially

After escaping the police, Marv ditches his car. From *Sin City: The Hard Goodbye*. Art by Frank Miller. Copyright © Frank Miller, Inc.

when it isn't providing the moment with any added flair. In the film, the narration simply continues over the cut. It doesn't coincide with any particular moment where Marv becomes more resolute in his desire to bring about justice or deal out punishment, so the rapid shift in perspective feels clunky and arbitrary rather than essential. The comic's transition feels more graceful, and this likely occurs because, on the page, it reads more like a slow push in toward the character rather than an abrupt cut in. Since a comic can't actually make a character slowly grow larger in only two panels, Miller's choices were either to use a large number of smaller panels to give the effect of a slow push in, or to use two larger panels with the two more extreme images in them, trusting that the reader understands the transition. Miller picked the more spartan approach of two images, a logical choice because the focus of the scene isn't on the action of swimming. The film, however, could have easily used a push in that slowly brought the viewer toward Marv. This would have created a slower, even pace to the scene that would have effectively highlighted the narration while allowing the technique of the filmmaking to recede into the background of the scene. Instead, by choosing to exactly replicate the choices of the comic, the film actually feels less graceful than the source material and creates an awkward moment in the flow of the action where there had previously been only fluid storytelling.

The one concern that seems to continually pop up in these comparisons is the way that film moves inextricably forward while comics present frozen moments in time. Films place one moving image after another and sweep the viewer along a predetermined path for a predetermined amount of time. Comics simply cannot exert this level of control over their readers and a successful comic creator must keep this fact in mind. It is useful to examine moments where film's primary tools, structure and editing, and a comics' layout collide to see exactly how the film and the comic craft similar sequences.

A good sequence to look at for this comparison comes fairly late in each version of the story. It's a short sequence where Marv is preparing to take on Kevin, the man who carried out Goldie's murder. Here, Marv goes over the supplies he put together for the task, and the way that each medium represents these items implicates differing storytelling possibilities. In the comic, the sequence takes place in the middle of a page and is comprised of ten panels in total. The panels are built with a slim but tall shot of Marv's face to the left and a three by three grid to the right that features one item per panel. The layout is exceedingly regimented and does an excellent job of giving the feeling of a man ticking off a list in his head. It can easily be read in the traditional manner of left-to-right, then top-to-bottom, and ends with the dialogue, "and my mitts" placed in the bottom right of the grid (intended to be read last).[3] What is interesting about this panel structure, however, is that while there is a natural reading order, it is also meant to be seen as a whole. Placing Marv in a large slender panel to the left of the grid makes him a presence that is always felt on the periphery of the reader's vision and the grid structure gives a sense of Marv's regimented, clear thinking about the objects. The comic utilizes these tools to make sure the reader is paying attention to Marv's thought process and does it purely through a design decision that is available only to comics.

The film takes this grid and structures it as nine back-to-back shots that are set against a pure black background, the same visual choice made in the comic. It also orders them rigidly by keeping the length of each shot nearly identical. The sequence lasts for roughly nine seconds and each shot takes up about one second of screen time. This clear, balanced rhythm to the shots alongside Marv's matter-of-fact narration accomplishes a similar effect as the regimented grid does. The sequence creates a feeling of a man who is organized and set on his task, checking to make sure that nothing he needs has been forgotten. Marv's narration from the comic is replicated verbatim in the film and his voice propels the scene along as well as supports the same grim determination as his gritty countenance when seen out of the corner of the reader's eye.

Even with these similarities, both versions of this scene do an excellent job of stylizing the material in ways that are uniquely suited to their own medium. The comic uses a notably starker visual style than the film. Miller frequently wipes out all of the details of his images in the comic, leaving only black and white outlines that suggest items and characters to the reader. He employs such a technique here, leaving white spaces representing the objects against a completely pitch-black background. The film sometimes dabbles in this high-contrast imagery, like the opening scene which punctuates a kiss at a key moment. But the film does not employ it as frequently as the comic. This is because it's simply more jarring to do so in a film, where the images naturally feature a high level of detail that flesh and blood actors bring to an image. Illustration can readily suggest real life but it does so by portraying abstractions.

---

[3] Miller, Frank. *Sin City*. Milwaukie, OR: Dark Horse Comics, 2001. Page 162.

So when the comic takes a further step toward abstraction and away from reality, it's a smaller step taken, whereas a live-action film takes a step toward that same heightened level of abstraction and strains. The pure black background in the film does enough to offset the image from the "reality" of *Sin City*'s world that it isn't necessary to completely white out the objects as well. While this is one of the major differences between the two scenes, the film also tosses in a couple extra flourishes that are simply unavailable to a comic: sound effects. (The cocking of a pistol is inserted over the shot of a gun, and the final image of Marv's hands is accentuated as they move down to the center of the frame and tremble with fury.) Each depiction is fairly similar when compared to one another, but the small touches of style that differentiate them speak volumes about just how different the tools available to each medium are.

The final comparison I'd like to make is between two versions of a scene that focuses on dialogue. The film version of the scene was guest-directed by Quentin Tarantino, and it's stylistically different from the rest of the film; it's not entirely clear what influence Miller might have exerted over the sequence, if any. It's a unique dialogue sequence in that one of the participants is actually dead, but it features a back and forth dialogue between two characters in a single location and illustrates the ways that film and comics keep a conversation-heavy scene moving. It's easy to make a brawl look dynamic but what about two talking heads? How do these concerns affect the two media?

The third volume of the series, subtitled *The Big Fat Kill*, features another story that was integrated into the *Sin City* movie. It takes place during the middle of the overall running time and the conversation is between Dwight, a rough and tumble outsider who is trying to help the prostitutes of Sin City, and Jackie Boy, a now deceased cop who was killed while making an unwelcome pass at one of the prostitutes on their home turf of Old Town. Dwight is spiriting Jackie Boy's remains to the tar pits to hide the body, but since Jackie Boy's equally dead cronies took up all the trunk space, Dwight was forced to place the body in the front seat. Dwight's anxious nerves bring Jackie Boy back to life, even if only in his mind, as Dwight plays out a fevered and worried conversation about the danger he is in.

Both sequences start out with a roughly identical shot of the car being driven straight toward the viewer. The composition of the comic features a slightly lower angle but the shots are still close enough in composition and presentation that they're essentially identical in their effect on the audience.

The true separation point between the two images is that the film blows out the headlights on the car, pushing the brightness of each headlight to a point where everything in a small radius around them is overtaken by a white-out effect. The comic features no such effect. Instead, the salient, stylistic detail of the page is the stark contrast between the pitch-black background and the completely white daggers of rain that slice toward the ground. In the film, the rain is still present, but it is a detail of the shot rather than a true focal point of the image. The film is less likely to abstract its images into a pure black and white contrast than the comic, and by restricting this stylistic decision, the film has to find other ways to stimulate visuals when it cannot follow the comic's lead. The film still uses the contrast of a bright light against a darker image but it finds another element of the scene to bolster the contrast: the bright white headlights, specifically an element that would be realistically plausible. Therefore the film likely holds back from the stark black and white imagery the comic favors simply because it would feel too unrealistic when compared to the more detailed images that live action filming captures.

As the scene continues, the film connects two panels from the comic with a track to the left. The movement is fluid and slow and has a similar effect to the comic presenting two panels. The only difference is that the comic uses this second panel to set off the rest of the scene in a more restrained style. The first image of the car, which helps to establish the setting, is presented at a slightly low angle in a full page spread with a long white rectangle running down the side featuring Dwight's narration. It's a unique-looking panel that draws attention to its layout and stylistic properties. The next panel is a half-page image establishing the flow of the rest of the sequence. Nearly every page of this conversation features either two or three panels. (There are a pair of exceptions to this rule of only two to three panels per page, but the layout seeks to preserve this general construction during the deviations by keeping the offending panels at the same height as the panels preceding them, preserving the overall presentation when a reader looks at the whole page.) Because of this, the reader is able to ease smoothly from the dynamic opening shot outside the car into the measured pace of the rest of the sequence, which takes place inside the automobile.

This style has another effect in the film, though. The first shot within the car groups Jackie Boy and Dwight, Jackie on the left and Dwight on the right. The orientation of the initial shot preserves the same diagonal framing that was

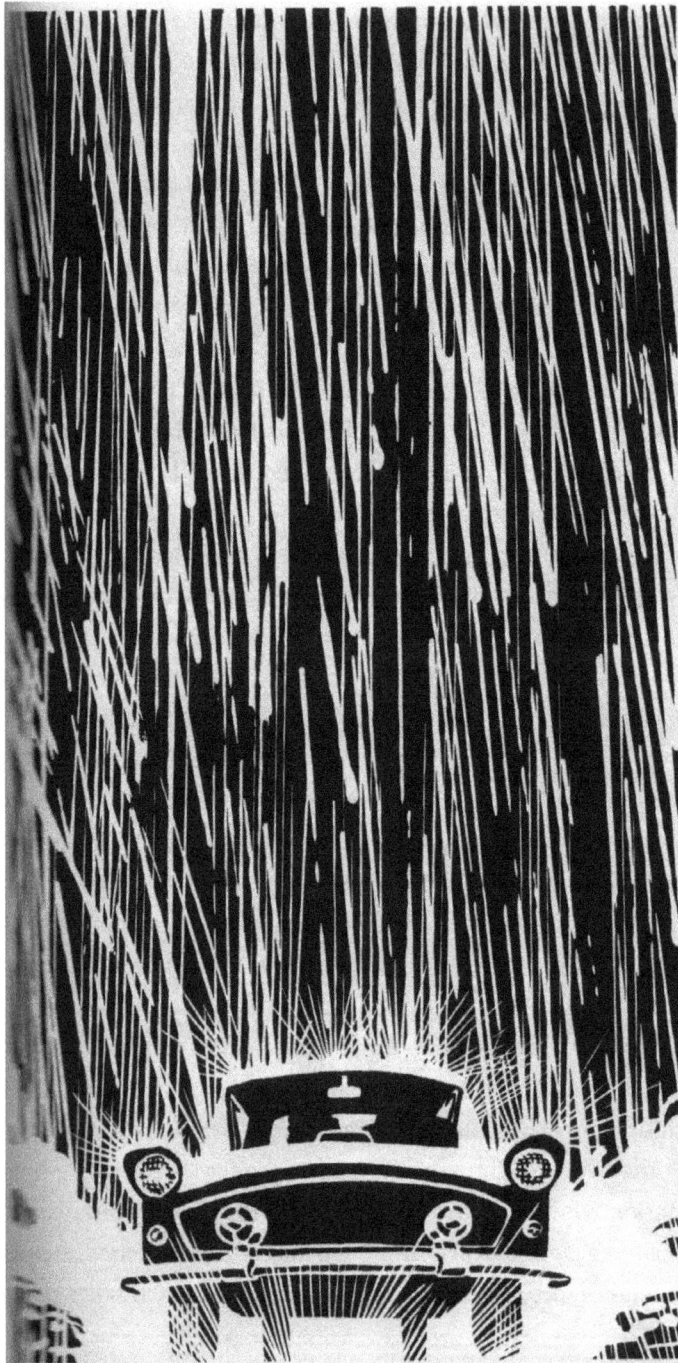

DIZZY DAMES. WHAT WERE THEY *THINKING,* STICKING ME WITH A BEAT-UP BUCKET OF BOLTS LIKE THIS? SOMEBODY OUGHTTA TAKE IT OUT BACK AND *SHOOT* IT. IT'D BE A *MERCY.*

A FEW YEARS BEFORE I WAS *BORN,* THIS T-BIRD MUST'VE BEEN A PRETTY SWEET SET OF WHEELS. BUT IT'S BEEN AROUND A FEW TOO MANY BLOCKS A FEW TOO MANY TIMES AND WHOEVER OWNED IT OBVIOUSLY DIDN'T INDULGE IN LUXURIES LIKE THE OCCASIONAL TUNE-UP OR OIL CHANGE. THE ENGINE JERKS AND FARTS LIKE AN OLD MAN ON A BAD DIET. THE STEERING MECHANISM'S GOT TERMINAL ARTHRITIS. THE SUSPENSION MAKES EVERY POTHOLE AN ADVENTURE. THE LEFT REAR TIRE IS AS SOFT AS A ROTTEN BANANA AND IF THAT'S A SLOW LEAK I'M GOOD AND SCREWED. I HAD TO CHUCK THE SPARE TO MAKE ROOM FOR ALL THE NEATLY CHOPPED BODY PARTS WE PACKED IN THE TRUNK.

MAYBE FIVE BLOCKS OUT I HAPPEN TO GLANCE DOWN AT THE GAS GAUGE. WHAT I SEE GETS ME POUNDING MY FISTS AGAINST THE STEERING WHEEL LIKE SOME LUNATIC. I CURSE OUT EVERY GIRL WHO EVER WORKED OLD TOWN AND EVERY RELATIVE ANY OF THEM EVER HAD.

HOW THE HELL AM I SUPPOSED TO MAKE IT ALL THE WAY TO THE PITS AND BACK ON LESS THAN AN EIGHTH OF A TANK?

DIZZY DAMES! DIZZY, SCARED, STUPID DAMES! YOU COULDN'T BOTHER TO FILL THE GOD DAMN GAS TANK?

The stylized comic book goes to extremes of high contrast that the movie doesn't. From *Sin City: The Big Fat Kill.* Art by Frank Miller. Copyright © Frank Miller, Inc.

SETTLE DOWN. GET RATTLED AND YOU'RE NO USE TO ANYBODY. BREATHE STEADY. BREATHE DEEP. ALL YOU NEED IS LUCK. A LOT OF LUCK. GREAT, BIG, FAT GOBS OF LUCK. AN ACT OF GOD WOULDN'T HURT A BIT.

I CAN'T STOP FOR GAS. I CAN'T STOP FOR ANYTHING. I CAN'T GET STOPPED FOR ANYTHING.

NOT WHILE I'M HAULING HUNDREDS OF POUNDS OF THE WRONG KIND OF MEAT.

NOT WITH THE PASSENGER I'VE GOT RIDING SHOTGUN.

MY FELLOW TRAVELER.

WE RAN OUT OF ROOM. WE WERE BARELY ABLE TO GET THE TRUNK TO STAY CLOSED AS IT WAS. WE'D PACKED IT SO TIGHT. TWO OF THE GIRLS HAD TO SIT ON THE LID BEFORE I COULD GET THE LOCK TO CATCH.

AND THERE WAS JACKIE-BOY, LEFT OVER.

IF THIS HEAP WAS A FOUR-SEATER, WE COULD'VE TOSSED HIM IN THE BACK. BUT THERE WASN'T ANYTHING WE COULD DO BUT PILE HIM IN RIGHT NEXT TO ME, OUT WHERE ANYBODY WHO CARES TO LOOK WILL SEE HIM.

GO AHEAD. HELP YOURSELF TO ONE OF HIS CIGARETTES. IT'LL HELP.

GO AHEAD. IT'LL HELP.

After the previous page's establishing shot, the story moves inside the car. From *Sin City: The Big Fat Kill.* Art by Frank Miller. Copyright © Frank Miller, Inc.

created by moving to the left of the car in the shot that preceded it. The film establishes an outward view that looks in on the car and then moves inside the vehicle while retaining the same perspective on the characters and setting as the outward view. Would it have been jarring to move from a head-on shot of the car into an angled interior shot? Perhaps not, but doing so would likely break the slow rhythm of the scene. The film isn't trying to punctuate this specific moment with a flashy show of style, so it connects two shots together with a similar orientation toward the characters within the scene, in order to help ease the transition into the car. In doing so, it eliminates a panel. The transition in the comic from outside to inside the car takes place from the same angle as the film does, but in the comic iteration, Miller instead chooses to cut to a straight-on shot of Dwight hunched over the wheel. He then transitions into the two shot of Jackie Boy and Dwight, at the top of the next page. Why did Miller make this decision to withhold Jackie Boy from the first panel? Miller wanted to establish the rhythm of panels discussed earlier while still holding off on Jackie Boy's appearance as an active member of the scene. (The dialogue presented on the next page comes in tandem with Jackie Boy's first appearance.) Dwight's narration on the second page is again run in a long white box down the right of the page and at the bottom of the first panel, he specifically mentions Jackie. In doing so, Miller withholds Jackie Boy's presence from the reader until they read these words, forcing him to come up with another image to fill the bottom half of the first page where no narration is featured. He could have cut out the first of these two pages entirely, but doesn't. He eases the reader into the sequence and his use of a panel featuring just Dwight showcases how he dances around the pressures that comics place on him as he guides a reader through the story. Obviously, the film didn't have to deal with these restrictions, and so it is able to excise the shot of Dwight clutching at the wheel because its images aren't tethered to a specific location on a page.

The next few panels commence in similar manner to the film, but also highlight a few changes made to the sequence. The film adds splashes of colored light that bounce through the window, bathing the screen in alternating colors such as green, red, orange, and blue. It's an artistic augmentation on behalf of the filmmaker, despite the restraint exercised by the comic with its use of color in general. The first appearance of color in *Sin City* is in the fourth volume, *That Yellow Bastard*, where the titular Bastard bore a stark jaundiced hue in every panel he graced. The film uses that specific stylistic choice as well but applies it to the other stories in the film too, placing bold reds and other colors in the frame more frequently to highlight certain portions. Part of the reason for the decision to make such an overt use of color in this scene is likely because the film cannot easily abstract its images through stark black and white in the same way that the comic can. This scene in the comic is particularly notable for highlighting some very abstract uses of this contrast, and while the film makes some allusions to this technique—Benicio del Toro's blood makeup for instance glows a bright, pure, white—it can't come close to what the comic presents. Instead the film decides to use a shifting, playful splash of color that constantly changes. It fits well with film's ability to accurately display time by allowing the changes to subtly morph one into the other and reflect what's outside the car at any given moment. The effect gives the car forward momentum since it's implied that the lights are caused by signs and other light sources that the car is passing. It strengthens the film more so than a similar technique would in a comic because it can alter the coloring within a single shot. In a comic, it would be harder to discern the actual source of the lighting since there would be only one major color choice over each panel. Certainly it wouldn't be impossible to divine what was causing these new colors to be added to the scene, but having swathes of green cover one panel and then orange in the next would likely be harder to comprehend as an environmental effect of the comic's setting. The film's ability to consistently and repeatedly change small aspects of a single shot in real time allows it to experiment in ways that would prove difficult for a comic, just as the comic is able to deploy abstracted imagery which escapes the scope of filmic realism.

Another important alteration between the two media is the manner in which the film portrays Jackie Boy in this sequence. The comic gives Jackie Boy some movement and expression. He's not simply a voice coming out of an inanimate object, but the comic's interpretation never comes anywhere near the level of movement that the film utilizes. This isn't all that surprising since the majority of the changes concerning the film adaptation embody the notion that film is a medium composed of moving images, but it's worth noting once more for the additions and alterations it brings to the scene. In fact, the moment Jackie Boy stirs he is without dialogue. The film cuts in to a close up of Jackie Boy's head as he slowly begins to look over at Dwight. For a few seconds Jackie Boy wordlessly looks at Dwight as a discordant sound plays on the score to accentuate the change in the scene. Motion and sound carry the shock of Jackie Boy's sudden re-animation while the comic focuses on a different tactic to help carry this shock. The moment in the comic when Jackie first speaks is delayed until it can be placed as the first panel on the left side of the page and shows Jackie Boy displaying a facial expression that appears somewhere between a yell and a demonic possession. Jackie Boy looks extremely menacing in the comic, while in the film he's fairly calm and collected. (The simple act of moving his dead flesh implies the menace.) The comic and film both portray this as an important, dramatic moment that needs to be punctuated, using the unique tools each medium possesses. Throughout the rest of the film scene, Jackie Boy's head bobs and lolls as he delivers his dialogue, accentuating both the fact that he's dead and the way his neck has been almost completely severed. It even affects the way del Toro chooses to deliver his dialogue. When Jackie Boy's head slides backward and exposes his gaping neck wound, he accentuates his performance with a raspy, barely audible vocal inflection. Here the motion added to the sequence changes the actual reading of the dialogue, a direct result of translating this page to the screen. Comics also have tools that can reflect different kinds of speech; specific fonts or alterations in the size of text lend themselves to focusing the reader on how the words are "actually" being spoken. None of these tools are utilized in this scene, however, highlighting the fact that this change came about wholly because of the added movement that film brought to this particular depiction of the action.

The film does more to separate itself from the comic than just highlighting character motion; one of the major stylistic additions to this scene is that of camera zooms. The scene is playing with a tense, volatile situation and one of the ways that Tarantino chooses to showcase this fact is by having the camera zoom in on characters as they speak or as they process information. Going back to the first moment when Dwight realizes that Jackie Boy is speaking to him, we see a snap zoom that punctuates the sudden comprehension of his fragile mental state. After the close up on Jackie Boy, the camera cuts out to a two shot of Jackie Boy and Dwight. The moment Jackie Boy's line delivery finishes, the camera zooms in on the pair, framing Dwight tightly on the edge of the shot, accompanying this with a subtle whooshing sound. The movement of the scene from reality to hallucination is clearly marked by both motion and sound. The film knows how to deploy its tools to guide the viewer through the story much like the comic knows how to do so by deploying exaggerated facial expressions and specific panel placements. In the rest of this scene multiple types of zooms are used: snap zooms for moments of heightened emotion and slow, subtle zooms to highlight the escalating pressure and intensity that Dwight is feeling as the seconds tick by. Almost all of the changes in this sequence can be traced back to the simple fact that film portrays actual motion while comics do not. By deploying techniques specific to filmmaking, the film takes the particular scene and presents it in a manner that intends to elicit the same effects as the comic, but accomplishes this in a different fashion. The comic knows how to tell its story and how to make use of the tools the medium provides and therefore presents an exciting, tense scene.

Clearly, the most consistent creative deviations presented in the adaptation of *Sin City* were impacted by the film's ability to portray actual motion. Movement, and the way that film features a locked, linear progression of events, influenced many of the storytellers' decisions, and in doing so created a very specific version of the story that differed in both subtle and overt ways from the comic-book source. So was Rodriguez's claim that he was trying to make a film into a comic justified? Not entirely; *Sin City* certainly makes some bold visual choices and at times looks nearly identical to its comic counterpart, but ultimately the way the movie was designed plays in a way that is primarily similar to other films. The film is still successful at telling its story, and while its look may be inspired by the *Sin City* comics, the nuts and bolts are that of the medium of film. Rodriguez and Miller were clever enough to realize that this had to be the case if they were going to make a movie that functioned as anything more than animated comic panels.

A Moving *Persepolis*

The comic *Persepolis* is a memoir; in it Marjane Satrapi details the trials of daily life growing up in Iran during revolution and war while under an oppressive regime. *Persepolis* was originally published in the English language by a division of Random House called Pantheon (after its French publication by L'Association); this is interesting because it is a comic that was published, in English at least, by a traditional book publisher. The first of the two volumes was released in 2003 and this says much about the legitimacy that comics had accrued by this point in time. *Persepolis* was seen as a work of art that could stand in comparison to traditional novels and its release by a respected book publisher attests that comics had indeed become a respected art form. The comic was released to notable acclaim, landing an extremely favorable review from *Time Magazine*[1] and ending up on its list of top 10 best comics of the year.[2] A film adaptation produced by notable industry talent Kathleen Kennedy in 2007 traveled a similar path to both its audience and acclaim. It was made and released in France and then moved abroad, again receiving positive reviews, one of course from *Time* magazine,[3] and wound up on *Time*'s list for

---

[1] Arnold, Andrew. "An Iranian Girlhood." web.archive.org/web/20030622094439/http://www.time.com/time/columnist/arnold/article/0,9565,452401, 00.html (accessed 24 Feb 2009).

[2] Arnold, Andrew. "The Best Comix." time.com/time/bestandworst/2003/comics.html (accessed February 24, 2009).

[3] Corliss, Richard and Mary. "*Persepolis* Finds Love in the Afternoon." time.com/time/arts/article/0,8599,1624714,00.html (accessed 24 Feb 2009).

top 10 movies of the year,[4] bypassing old notions that animated films are inherently more childish than live action films. The film and the comic have similar goals, and it shows. More interestingly, both were created in a form that had previously been dismissed as less artistic and less important culturally and yet still managed to succeed from a critical standpoint. The works are not identical, though, and the fact that there are plenty of changes made to the material in the process of adaptation is what makes the two works useful in further analysis.

Satrapi co-directed the film version of *Persepolis*, so it's safe to assume that her goals and storytelling sensibilities affected the creation of both works in similar ways. Satrapi, of course, had less control over the film than she had over the comic, due to the nature of creating films, which more or less necessitates a collaborative creative process. Most telling, however, is that Satrapi did not wish to take on the job of directing the film alone. She understood that creating a film was not analogous to creating a comic and brought on a seasoned creator of animated works to help her avoid the pitfalls of a new medium. In moving *Persepolis* from the page to the screen, new artistic hurdles would be encountered while new storytelling possibilities would also emerge. Satrapi herself explains, "People generally assume that a graphic novel is like a movie storyboard, which of course is not the case. With graphic novels, the relationship between the writer and reader is participatory. In film, the audience is passive. It involves motion, sound, music, so therefore the narrative's design and content is very different."[5] It's difficult to generalize that comics involve more participation than film, but as a baseline for modern, mainstream filmmaking versus modern mainstream comic book creation, this statement rings true. Ultimately, the translation to film utilized all these new tools Satrapi mentioned to help tell the story, but the most important addition was that of movement. Satrapi, her co-director Vincent Paronnaud, and all of their collaborators expertly configure the story of *Persepolis* to take advantage of the tool of motion, one that the comic version could not use.

---

[4] Corliss, Richard. "Top 10 Movies." time.com/time/specials/2007/top10/article/0,30583,1686204_1686244_1692014,00.html (accessed 14 Feb 2009).

[5] Payvand News. "Interview with Marjane Satrapi – Director / Author of *Persepolis*." payvand.com/news/07/dec/1254.html (accessed 3 Jan 2009).

As the previous studies concluded, there are moments when the two pieces coincide and utilize similar techniques to convey the same emotions or to affect the viewer in a comparable fashion. Ultimately, these are the product of creative choices on behalf of Satrapi and her co-director Paronnaud. In many of the examples I will explore, scenes are changed when a direct translation could occur. Why, in an adaptation that was created by the same author, would this be the case? Two distinct versions of *Persepolis* emerge resulting from the adaptation from print to film, primarily via the implementation of motion in the narrative. This chapter will further explore the addition of motion to *Persepolis*, a work that originated in a static medium, as well as a variety of choices that were made in the processes of adaptation. Examining a few scenes in detail demonstrates how Satrapi drastically altered her basic methods of storytelling in order to best preserve the original intent of their work.

As the film version of *Persepolis* opens, it is easy to see how motion has been injected into the piece. As the credits roll, images, like paper cutouts from a comic book, are slowly pushed left and right. Waves of water move up and down in rows with lo-fi charm characteristic of simple stage plays with cardboard sets. The motion is surreal, an animated collage of the arabesque, and minimal in comparison to the majority of the film, but one aspect the credit sequence carries is a focused implementation of motion akin to later scenes in the film. Flower petals flow across many of the relatively static (in composition) frames. The petals even flow across credits at times, prompting a reading order, a task that is often accomplished in comics through page layouts. (These flowers that drift around the scene eventually become a motif in the film. We see them occur again when Marjane repeats the story about how her grandmother places flower petals in her bra as a kind of perfume. They also return at the end of the film when we are told that Marjane's grandmother is dead.) This combination of art design merged with intentional motion neatly illuminates symbolic plot elements and indicates where the film diverges from its source material. The wavering cardboard pieces comprising the scene evoke an unnatural two-dimensional image that imparts comic-book aesthetics, but does so through the tool of motion. On the other hand, the flower petals violate this artificial motion and flow through the paper arrangements with smooth, delicate movements, suggesting what the flowers represent while presenting a distinctly non-comics-like style of motion which will be picked up and utilized for the rest of the film. The film strives for fidelity to its source material by evoking the stasis of comics while transitioning into the full motion of cinema. It is useful, however, to compare this opening to the comic's opening to understand the difference.

The book's first page establishes a pattern of vignettes, comprising the foundations of the comic. The story is separated into a series of shorter stories, each with its own title that is comprised of a black rectangle with the title of the chapter on the right and a drawing of the chapter title to the left. The comic does not concern itself with a lyrical opening as the film does; it dives right into the story. Brief context is provided to establish the basic premise; for instance, a portrait of Satrapi as a ten year old with accompanying text to explain the year and what exactly is going on. Satrapi doesn't spend time establishing a specific mood as the credits of the film do; rather, she gives information about herself, her country, and the general timeframe in which the story is set. This informs the design of each work. The comic is a larger, sprawling piece that functions as a mosaic of stories, while the film collects these stories and reworks them into a single unified piece. The opening of the comic is less concerned with setting a general feeling and is focused on informing the reader and contextualizing the world of the comic. The film takes a different approach, founding the emotional mood as opposed to establishing an intellectual frame of mind. This does not mean that the film is more empathetic than the comic. The types of stories being told require different openings and each has a unique feel that is appropriate to the piece. The film version is notable because it immediately establishes itself in a fashion that at first seems to evoke a comic but then is quickly transformed by the integration of motion. The film's opening pays tribute to its origins but does so in a way that is uniquely filmic, bending motion to both evoke a medium that cannot utilize movement while also presenting a distinctly filmic style of movement. This decision speaks both to the shift in media and to the fact that the film is not an original piece of work, so, while it is telling the story in a way that the comic does not, it is still thinking about the way a comic looks and how this can be represented in a film.

The comic establishes itself through a realistic, anthropological approach, so much so that the second panel is explained as a photo of Satrapi's class, one in which only a sliver of Marjane's veil is visible. The work drives a world-building narrative, aiming to present a clearer picture of Iran and the world at this time while also telling Marjane's story. Particularly, this style favors context and slight diversions rather than a tightly woven story that fits into an hour and a half. A film could, of course, present a sprawling epic, but a mainstream feature film (the type of movie this book is examining) does not have the luxury of entertaining the long-winded digressions that the original comic pursues. This also reflects how comics can be read either in one sitting or over a period of time. A grouping of short stories is very conducive to a comic, while it is not as effective for a feature film. As such, two different styles of storytelling dominate the two works. But while each tells the same story, they diverge almost immediately.

Many scenes from the comic are carried over to the film with very few changes to the base content, but the ways that these scenes do diverge is essential to understanding the differing pressures that each medium exerts on the creative process. Examining a few select scenes that are similar in content and determining how and why they were changed in the move between media are the focus of this chapter. The first features the story of how the English intervened and helped create the Iranian dictatorship that is led by the Shah. Each version features Marjane's father telling her about Iran's past. The comic jumps back and forth between the present and the past frequently, whereas the film emphasizes a linear narrative, shifting to the past and telling the entirety of the history in a single compressed sequence. This focus dominates the stylized construction of the scenes. The comic features both a wide range of visual modifications: documentary-like panels, more overt "lighting," and changes in the presentation of speech balloons; while the film returns to an aesthetic that is reminiscent of the opening credits, presenting a clear shift in time frames and tone. The film augments the story for comedic effect and emphasizes the absurdity of the scene. On the other hand, the comic elicits a broader range of emotions from the reader. Many of these changes, of course, are made to better replicate a theatrical product familiar to the filmgoers. A less precise retelling of Iran's history would break the narrative momentum of the film, whereas the comic's entire structure is built in short blocks. So a digressive historical sequence that is homogenous fosters a tone conducive to the work. Here we see the story moving from a comic to a feature film and the story being altered to most effectively take advantage of the medium.

In the comic, the initial movement from the present to the past is marked by a change in lighting. The soon-to-be Shah and his inner circle are sitting around a fire and this causes a sharp shadow to be cast on the side of two of the characters' faces. This brand of chiaroscuro facial lighting appears very

Satrapi moves her narrative into the past through use of chiaroscuro lighting. From *The Complete Persepolis*. Art by Marjane Satrapi. Copyright © Marjane Satrapi.

rarely in the comic and here it is deployed to help mark the transition between the two spaces that are co-existing on the same page since the move from present to past takes place in roughly the bottom third of a page. This lighting is not consistent in every panel during the flashback, but established as a motif signaling the Shah. This is seen in the next two panels that feature two other historical figures, Gandhi and Ataturk, speaking about their feelings regarding republics. These panels return to a flatter facial lighting scheme that feature no obscuring shadows and place their figures in a documentary style "talking head" composition of a medium shot against a black background. After this, the book shifts back to the present where Marjane's father is still telling her about the past. This is handled in a series of three panels that are all roughly the same size and fit in a single row across the page. Here the focus is on Marjane's father and we see the lighting helping to draw the reader's attention to his face. An arc across the background of the panel separates an area of light from dark, the dark always on top with the light on bottom. This arc always intersects the father's neck, placing his white head in a dark area, ensuring contrast. Marjane appears in two of the three panels but she is always in the lower half of the image, and her white head always plays against a white background. She blends more effectively with her surroundings and is slightly less noticeable than her father. This establishes a reading order that consists of reading the father's dialogue, then observing him, and finally looking at Marjane. This also strengthens the composition. The order also describes the construction of each panel from top to bottom, with words on top, the father below the words, and Marjane at the bottom of the panel (if she happens to be in the panel at all). Satrapi constructs the image so that natural contrasts (the white of the word balloon against the dark background is essentially the same as the whiteness of the father's head against this same background) are linked with the information that is traditionally read first, drawing the eye forward.

As the comic moves back into the past in the next panel, we see a panel that looks like a photo of Reza, the soon-to-be Shah, outlined in an oval of white and embedded in black. Here is another example of a panel becoming similar to a preserved document, just like the second panel of the book that featured a picture of Marjane's class. This "document" breaks from the traditional story panels the reader is used to and marks a shift in timeframe. Satrapi deftly uses the unconventional panel to convey to the reader that a narrative shift has occurred. Therefore, Satrapi molds this panel to alert the reader to a shift in the story while giving them an image that is nostalgic and embedded in history. Another example depicts the Shah being presented in a full body portrait much like a photo, something that represents the past. We have not yet seen a consistent method for noting this shift from past to present, but we have seen demarcations of this shift both times we have entered the past in this sequence. The next panel features two British aristocrats sitting while drinking, smoking, and talking about Reza and his rebellion. Their entire conversation fits in this panel, in a series of five separate word balloons, one on top of the other. All of these word balloons are individual units and are unconnected to any of the other ones, unlike most comics where all the word balloons that contain one character's dialogue in a panel represent a complete thought. Here Satrapi makes the two characters speak in short, staccato bursts, representing this through unconnected dialogue balloons. This is a rarity for *Persepolis* since it is usually typified by characters speaking in a single bubble regardless of how much text will have to fit within it. Satrapi consequently plays these bits of dialogue with a mocking tone. By splitting them into small bursts, it breaks the natural flow of comic dialogue and encourages a style of reading which helps ensure the comedic effect that Satrapi intends.

After this panel, we shift to a page where one of the aristocrats seduces Reza into abandoning the concept of a republic in favor of becoming an emperor. The first four panels are roughly similar in size and each features the aristocrat moving around Reza while telling him about why it is a better idea to become an emperor than to allow a republic to form. The first two panels feature a return of the strong facial lighting that marked the first panel and help to re-establish the space. The first real change on this page comes with the fifth panel: it is noticeably smaller and more vertically oriented than any of the previous panels on the page. The panel itself depicts the aristocrat's face at the top right looking down at Reza's face in the bottom left. The panel highlights how the aristocrat is seducing Reza and uses his height to help emphasize his power over Reza; furthermore, the panel also breaks the flow of previous panels and highlights an emotional shift in the page, letting the reader know that Reza is beginning to believe the aristocrat. By altering the panel size, Satrapi mimics the shift in Reza's thinking.

The seventh and eighth panels have a horizontal orientation, and feature the aristocrat explaining exactly what Reza needs to do to become an emperor. In the initial panel, the aristocrat assures Reza that he will not have to do

Satrapi uses panel size to reflect content and even characters' shifts of mentality. From *The Complete Persepolis*. Art by Marjane Satrapi. Copyright © Marjane Satrapi.

anything, and the following panel features the aristocrat with his arm around Reza. The aristocrat tells him that, as long as Reza secures the English his oil, they will take care of everything. Each like-sized panel highlights the duplicity of the aristocrat. Identical in size, the panels are situated one on top of the other, and feature indistinct landscapes in the background. Satrapi hammers home the point with the parallel construction of these panels, enhancing the naïveté of Reza's trust in the lecherous Western powers. These horizontal panels then lead the reader's focus to the third panel on the page, a roughly square panel that returns to Marjane's home and signals a shift in the story's narrative. It is not an emotional beat like the previous break in panel size we examined but transitions the flow of the narrative out of the past and into the present. Since Satrapi is using a consistent art style to depict the past and the present, she deploys a variety of stylistic techniques to help mark moments when the story is shifting timeframes. In this case a shift in panel shape allows Satrapi to highlight one of these changes for the reader.

The version of this scene in the film has a few striking differences, though, and features a variety of techniques that would be impossible to render with comic-book techniques. The film narrative is told in its entirety, without breaking away from the "historical world" that is presented. The comic fractures the story in multiple ways, telling it in two chunks spanning two consecutive chapters and moving between the past and the present during the father's retelling of the past. The film version eschews this idea in favor of an accelerated, focused telling of the tale. The transition to the past in the film begins as Marjane's father begins his story. The shot where this occurs features Marjane and her father sitting on a sofa in their house. As he begins to talk, the two separate and slowly slide toward their respective sides of the frame and begin to dissolve away. As this occurs, a stage begins to emerge out of the darkness of the background that used to be the family's house. The transition from present to past is distinct and clear, especially when curtains open up over the stage where the past will unfold. Motion is one of the key aspects of this change. Marjane and her father's unnatural slide out of frame, as well as the dramatic flourish of the curtains being pulled back, cue the viewer to notice the shift in the story's location, establishing a break between the two time frames in the film.

Also important to note is that once the curtains have been pulled back and the location established, the façade of the stage slides off-screen, leaving an ornately decorated background that features an art style reminiscent of the opening credits. Hills slowly shift in the background as the camera pushes in, initiating a fantastic departure from the stylized, but realistic, animation style that accompanies the majority of the film's story. When Reza glides into the frame, though, his motion is immediately striking and recognizable. His character's arms and body flail about from the inertia of his motion, replicating the movement of a cardboard stick puppet. When he turns around, his character reveals himself as a two dimensional figure, for a moment, intimating visually that these moments are fantastic and imbued with symbolism. Satrapi and her co-director completely alter their aesthetic for this sequence, overhauling the general design, the movement of characters, and even the tone (this sequence takes on a heavily comic air). Because the film is a single unbroken unit, Satrapi is able to push select aspects of particular scenes to greater levels of abstraction. We do not hop back and forth between the more morose present and the oddly comic past, and because of this there isn't a strange contrast between the two decidedly different locations. Similarly, the odd motions of the characters and the aesthetic of the sequence come into existence gradually, through a slow dissolve and an opening of curtains, signaling the shift from one space to another. Satrapi and Paronnaud use filmic techniques such as dissolves to help guide the viewer through the dissonant sequence in the film. By minimizing contrast through cinematic techniques such as dissolves, the creators successfully shift the scene, allowing the viewer to accept the transition.

Motion is one of the defining components of this version of the sequence. The comedic tone results largely from the absurd way that the characters move. The aristocrat literally pops into frame in a puff of smoke and slides around Reza, at one point entering from the top right of a frame with his head facing toward the ground and at other times descending toward the ground as if he were on some sort of off-screen elevator. It is easy to see how this sequence builds itself around a property that comics have no access to, and how the decision to build it around comical movement necessitates that it isolate itself from other portions of the film. While movement is one of the major aspects of this sequence, it is also worth noting how sound production carries the scene. The way in which characters deliver their lines during this sequence is hyperbolic, especially one moment where Marjane accuses Reza of being a "moron" and suddenly he and all his followers look directly at the camera and exclaim "ooooohhhhhhh." (Whether or not French is the viewer's native language, how the line is delivered communicates humor.)

Unlike the comic's version of the past, which is intertwined with the present due to a less centralized location in the narrative, the film's version is boiled down and focused into one minute and twenty-three seconds of screen time. This unified approach then singles out a particular aspect of the sequence (the comedy), which prompts stylistic changes that distinguish it from the rest of the film. The comic version could attempt to portray a more comedic tone—a shift in art style or a change in the font of the lettering could accomplish this task—but if the same aesthetics of interwoven interludes remained, it would cause a clash between the mingling time periods. The adaptation of the scene into a portion of a feature film, a style of filmmaking that cannot afford the longer, more leisurely pace of the original piece, necessitated this switch to a more focused sequence. This allowed a complete shift in how the scene was constructed even if the same information was relayed to the audience.

The two scenes provide unique perspectives on the same basic material. In the comic we see a digressive and complex story structure, while the film features a tight, focused telling of Iran's history. The same principals are executed across the work as a whole, and illustrate the unique ways the narrative is developed in each medium. Each piece, likewise, is altered stylistically to take advantage of the particular medium it's nested in. The comic shifts back and forth between time frames, but makes sure to signal these shifts clearly with unique panel types and subtle aesthetic alterations. The film also alters its aesthetics to mark shifts in time but it also utilizes movements and dissolves to help the viewer realize that a change in setting is about to occur. Aesthetic shifts such as changes in lighting or character design help to provoke a reader or viewer's attention. However, each medium can utilize a tool the other might not have access to, such as overt use of motion or a shift to a unique panel size that does not fit the traditional panel choices the comic is relying on. Both changes are not particularly foreign to fans of either medium, but each is just enough of an oddity to provoke attention from the intended audience and to indicate a change in timeframe. The respective media and the norms of each format help define storytelling methodology for either adaption.

The next scene is less of a departure from the source material. The telling of Iran's history yielded two drastically different presentations of the same material, but a sequence that features Marjane being stopped by two

"Guardians of the Revolution" after purchasing an outlawed cassette retains its structure and some aesthetic choices. Both versions of the sequence begin with Marjane walking down Gandhi Avenue amidst a crowd of street vendors surreptitiously hawking their music. The comic features a long horizontal panel comprised of seven vendors, each with a speech balloon indicating what they are selling. Marjane approaches the right side of the panel and is placed just to the left of the page's midpoint. The film utilizes a long shot with five vendors, two on the left of the frame and three on the right, with Marjane walking toward the right of the frame through the gap between them. As she walks, the five vendors all declare what they are selling. These two compositions compare rather favorably even if they are each subtly different. The comic's construction is built upon the way that a reader will scan the page. Marjane walks from left to right, the natural flow of reading, and the vendors are arranged in a straight line along the page. The film complicates the image slightly by placing vendors on either side of Marjane. This kind of composition is possible in film because Marjane's movement is not left up to the viewer and her character can easily move toward the camera. In a comic this kind of composition would likely have a tougher time conveying Marjane's movement even though her general direction is still from left to right. Comics lack the power of cinema to subject the viewer to the exact movement that is intended and the subtle differences in composition in these scenes emphasize how comics must be constructed in a way that is visually coherent for readers if they desire to successfully guide a reader through the story.

There is a slight deviation in the next portion of the scene. Following the long horizontal panel, Marjane tells the reader that she purchased two tapes in a narration box that is accompanied by a panel showing the street vendor she buys from. In this panel the street vendor is depicted as having two faces, one looking left and the other right. This is picked up in the next panel where Marjane has just received the tapes and now has two heads of her own, one looking in each direction. Satrapi is representing the caution of the two as they conduct their illegal transaction through physically impossible abstraction. This decision naturally arises from the inability to portray real motion, so in its place Satrapi draws some "movement lines," two dashes that follow the head as if it were actually moving, and puts two versions of a character's head in one panel, suggesting the motion that cannot be portrayed. The film actually adds a new portion of the story here. Marjane walks past the first set of street vendors, a

A young Satrapi is confronted by the Guardians of the Revolution. From *The Complete Persepolis*. Art by Marjane Satrapi. Copyright © Marjane Satrapi.

cut occurs and she walks by another, before off-screen sound alerts her to a new vendor who is selling just the tape she wants. She hears the cue, turns, and changes direction. This is followed by a cut and in the next shot Marjane is now seen walking from right to left. This addition is perfectly suited to the cinematic world. It would be easy for Marjane to simply walk up to a vendor after walking by a long row of other vendors and stop when she heard the name of the band she was looking for, but this might ultimately be boring. So Satrapi and Paronnaud decide to hinge the surprise on a haphazard discovery, utilizing off-screen space, off-screen sound, and a change in movement. The difference here is the use of right-to-left movement. In the comic the entire page features Marjane moving left to right, and this is a natural decision because a reader takes in the page from left to right. It wouldn't be inappropriate for Satrapi to utilize right-to-left motion in the comic, but it would bring unnecessary attention to the act of storytelling, and that is rarely the goal of the book. The shift in motion barely registers for a viewer of the film but the change is significant since it transitions from the market place to Marjane's discovery of the music she wants. Both sequences are executed in ways conducive to the medium's proper presentation, but each accomplishes the scene without calling attention to the artifice of their storytelling. Interestingly, though, each technique utilized is not entirely unique to the medium it is deployed in. Comics can utilize right-to-left movement and an animated, or live action, film can present a character's rapid movement as creating multiple heads. However, these storytelling techniques would be fundamentally altered if they shifted to a different medium. Right-to-left movement would likely be jarring for a reader and would upset the natural flow of a page that is built around left-to-right movement. Likewise, a character suddenly shaking his or her head so rapidly that it produces a second one would likely be at least mildly surprising in film. The two techniques are not specific to either comics or film but they must be deployed carefully in each medium; each is linked to the conventions of the story's formal construction. This pressures the creators to deploy the techniques in specific ways that will be most effective and can limit the choices available to a creator based solely on the medium they are working in.

The next portion of the scene also allows us to see how the film reconfigures the presentation of the story to focus on the motion of the characters. After Marjane drives down the price of the tape in a series of seven rapidly shifting close ups of her and the vendor (a sequence which plays much more swiftly and effectively on the screen than a series of seven panels could hope to play on the page), the movie cuts to the lower half of two black figures sliding across the street from right to left. These are the Guardians of the Revolution and in the comic they are introduced in a car driving through the background as Marjane, walking down the street, thinks about the tapes she just purchased. If the filmic composition was re-rendered and transformed into a comic panel, it would likely make little sense. It would merely be two black figures on a street with little context and it would be missing the ominous slithering sound effect that accompanies their entrance in the film. It is not out of the question that some readers would be able to infer that these are actually people clad in burkas, but then the creator would also have to contend with how to imply motion. Motion lines could help render movement through a panel, but another problem arises here: how would the reader know that these black shapes are coming after Marjane? The film utilizes the right-to-left movement to create awareness in the viewer that the shapes are headed in Marjane's direction. This version of *Persepolis* would have trouble making this right-to-left movement work without being slightly confusing because it violates the traditional left-to-right reading order. Satrapi could simply feature the black shapes moving from left to right and all would be fine, but this does not necessarily convince the audience that the threat is real. The power of these shapes in the film comes not from their depiction—they are not particularly terrifying—but from their slow and unnatural motion and the sliding hiss sound effect that accompanies them. Cinema alone can render the fear and aversion of Satrapi's rapacious theocratic wards, but the comic presents the Guardians in a car that is bearing down on Marjane, representing their character and intentions using static iconography. This doesn't mean that the comic is less provocative because the film plays more subtly with the Guardians' appearance, but only that the comic must effectively tell the story for an audience that relies heavily on stark visual clues to access the narrative. Both versions of *Persepolis* strive for clarity, and the choices made in each version of this scene speak to how clarity can be achieved.

Stopping her, the Guardians of the Revolution are next depicted questioning Marjane; they decide to bring her in until she tells a story of dread and woe, attempting to convince them to have mercy. Here, the largest change between the two sequences comes down to the depiction of the two Guardians. In the comic, they tend to be depicted as tall monoliths that make

Marjane look small in the panel, but in the film they are absurdly inhuman, with necks that stretch and move as if the pair were actually giraffes or eels. Once more, the film stylistically deploys ambient movement, highlighting the sudden and bizarre motions of the pair to exaggerate their cruelty. The comic manages this same feat, but it does it by emphasizing the oppressive nature of the pair. It focuses specifically on one of the Guardians, placing her exclusively on the left side of the panel and at one point leaving her face and placement in the panel unchanged for four consecutive images. This works well because it features a unique kind of panel transition that is largely eschewed in many mainstream comics—McCloud labels it a moment-to-moment transition—and this cues the reader to understand that only a small fraction of time has passed in between panels. This kind of panel is an oddity for many comics simply because utilizing it eats up a lot of page space. The less time that elapses between panels means more panels must be utilized to show small movements. As such, in a standard comic book, which features a limited 20 pages of story, moment-to-moment transitions are dangerous simply because they use a lot of page space for very little action. *Persepolis* is a longer story, so a moment-to-moment transition is not out of the question but it is largely left unused. By employing this static composition for the Guardian, Satrapi emphasizes her commitment to a technique that rapidly eats up space on the printed page while barely moving forward in the story. Each depiction strives to represent the power and cruelty that these women possess, but each interpretation makes unique choices about how to represent the story and these choices are heavily influenced by the medium in which the story is being told.

Nevertheless, there are similarities still between the two scenes. Two panels and two cuts in particular recall one another and seem to serve roughly the same purpose, but most interesting is a panel that contains a depiction of motion and a filmic action that seem to function the same way. First, as the Guardians examine Marjane, they call out two specific features of her outfit that worry them: her shoes and her Michael Jackson button. Each time they point to one of these aspects of her outfit the film cuts in to give a closer look at the offending item. The comic handles these moments in an identical fashion. The Guardians point out an item in one panel, and the next panel is composed to give a more specific view of said item. Then, when one of the Guardians pulls Marjane's scarf down, both the film and the comic execute the action similarly.

The confrontation with the Guardians of the Revolution continues. From *The Complete Persepolis*. Art by Marjane Satrapi. Copyright © Marjane Satrapi.

The confrontation with the Guardians of the Revolution concludes. From *The Complete Persepolis*. Art by Marjane Satrapi. Copyright © Marjane Satrapi.

The only difference is that the film's motion is more restrained in portraying the Guardian's forcefulness. The comic features the Guardian pulling Marjane's scarf in a fashion that covers her entire face. Motion lines are provided to highlight the action. Here, we see that motion is not solely the purview of film; the action shown in both versions is essentially identical. Since it doesn't move, The comic must be a bit more forceful to effectively get across the action, but the effect is ultimately the same, even if the exact depiction is slightly different. That said, different levels of intensity must be emphasized. Since comics do not have actual motion, exaggeration becomes a useful substitute.

The scenes diverge once more to showcase two entirely different versions of the same moment: Marjane must convince the Guardians not to take her in. She does this through the same method in each version by telling a sob story about her cruel stepmother. In the comic, this is shown through four panels where the Guardian and Marjane's positions remain constant while Marjane's facial expression moves from normal, to the verge of crying, to shedding a single tear, and finally to a stylistic abstraction of a weeping figure. This version of the scene uses panels that represent small portions of time to simulate minute changes in Marjane's facial expressions, which in turn helps to highlight her acting. The final panel of an overwrought Marjane putting on a face that looks quite bizarre is extremely effective at getting this notion across. The film also highlights Marjane's acting but does so in an entirely different fashion. As the pair grab Marjane and tell her she's coming with them, we see only Marjane against a wall of black fabric. Marjane begins to tell her story and the camera stays with her for a few moments, until overwrought music begins to swell in the background and the camera slowly tilts up, leaving Marjane behind. After a few moments of blackness we reach the Guardians' faces as Marjane's story continues. The scene culminates in the pair looking at each other and each changing their facial expressions to something resembling a lack of interest. At this moment, the two look to the left side of the frame and walk off, causing the phony music to warble out, calling attention to Marjane's acting much in the same way her unrealistic face did in the comic. Here we see the comic focusing on very specific depictions of Marjane over a series of moments, while the film plays more heavily with the tool of sound, featuring sound effects that would be impossible to effectively replicate in the purely visual realm of comics.

This scene also emphasizes the norms of each medium and the work itself; escalating tension and media-specific storytelling techniques are manipulated to produce a desired effect. The film relies heavily upon its musical score to present Marjane's lies while the comic utilizes a visually abstract style of depicting falsehood. Both of these stylistic decisions starkly differ from the way other scenes are approached in either work. Satrapi's comic is not overwhelmingly realistic in its depictions of humans but it has a set style that is based in reality and rarely altered. Thus, when she decides to make Marjane's face distort, as it does in this panel, it violates the norms that have been established so far in the work. The facial distortion is not, however, a departure from established visual tricks used in comic books. Considering the subject matter, and the tone of the work, it is not a jarring transition to see a drawn figure distort in this fashion. Instead it facetiously implies the insincerity of Marjane's plea to the Guardian. The facial distortion visually could strengthen the film's interpretation, especially with the depth and expressiveness afforded with animation. Interestingly, though, Satrapi and Paronnaud go in a different direction, relying on music to break down the stylized realism that the film aspires to emulate. The soundtrack swells and plays dramatic music that feels out of place. This sends the scene into the realm of melodrama and the music cues the viewer to assess Marjane's lies. The score, which is petulant, derivative, and stereotypical implies with irony the facetiousness of the emotions expressed in the isolated monologue. So, while the comic employs a technique that the film could replicate, the filmmakers depart from the comic, utilizing a technique that became available when the story was shifted from the world of comics to the world of film. This doesn't imply that film has more tools at its disposal and that this particular scene is creatively superior. In this instance the creative direction was reassessed to convey the plot in a universal way that most moviegoers would understand. Either version could have worked, but the comic artist and the film artists made separate choices that helped their stories thrive within their respective media, even if a more faithful translation was relatively accessible.

One small detail that brings motion back to the film and changes something from the comic remains to be discussed. Just before this sequence in the comic we see Marjane in her room in a panel featuring a poster of Iron Maiden and Marjane head-banging to music. Satrapi depicts this by featuring three different heads emerging from Marjane's body, which itself is slightly distorted as if it were in two separate positions. To fully sell the effect, Satrapi also adds in motion lines. The film also features Marjane head-banging to Iron Maiden, but moves the scene to the end while the comic uses a panel that features Marjane dancing to the music of Kim Wilde at the end of this sequence. This is a small change, but the film places the head-banging as the finale of this entire scene. The cathartic finale is an appropriate end to Marjane's awful day, effectively verbalized in her narration, "To each his own way of calming down."[6] Such commentary is absent during the film's iteration of Marjane's head-banging, and the viewer is meant to absorb her catharsis through visual and aural representations. While head-banging is successfully rendered in both media, film is able to extract more visceral emotion from it, owed to the movement and exuberant accompaniment played along with it. This enables the action to be placed in a location more significant to the overall narrative and focuses the scene sharply on the action. The comic, on the other hand, takes dancing and combines it with a jagged word balloon to indicate the volume of the music and narration. This does highlight the emotional significance of the scene just like the film, but does so in a way that doesn't rely as heavily on motion or sound. The ultimate difference is that the film manages to finish a scene with Marjane head-banging in her room along to the furious music of Iron Maiden and is therefore able to successfully complement the dramatic build of the scenes before. The comic on the other hand must rely on tools outside of motion and sound. A panel, or even a splash page, showing Marjane head-banging simply wouldn't be enough to close off this sequence because it and the jagged balloon would have a hard time accurately expressing Marjane's need to vent, so instead narration is added for clarity. The film's ability to present both motion and sound fluidly eliminates the need for narration, but the two carry emotion effectively and without dialogue from the characters.

The final comparison pertinent to this chapter comes from moments in the comic when Satrapi devotes large portions of a page to a single panel. These large panels themselves have a vast amount of flexibility, featuring many different depictions of time, motion, and story events. Some of these large panels were brought over into the film version of the story and these moments are worth looking at because the large panels themselves are rather striking images. They can arrest the viewer and invite them to pause for a moment so that they can fully take in the image presented. A larger panel cannot help but

---

[6] Satrapi, Marjane. *The Complete Persepolis*. United States: Pantheon Press, 2007. Page 134.

An example of large panels in *The Complete Persepolis*. Art by Marjane Satrapi. Copyright © Marjane Satrapi.

break the flow of a story unless the entire comic is told in this fashion. Since this is not the case in *Persepolis,* these larger panels immediately cause a reader to view them as important moments in the story, thus inviting more contemplation. Satrapi takes advantage of this by reserving large panels almost exclusively for moments that feature intensely emotional portions of the story. One instance of this sort of panel emerges when Marjane recalls that younger boys were told that if they died for Iran as martyrs they would go to Heaven. To represent this, they were given a "key to paradise" to wear around their necks. Satrapi features a panel that accounts for roughly two thirds of the entire page and shows a group of young boys with keys around their necks being killed by a violent explosion. One of the reasons that this is not a full-page spread is because Satrapi is showing how her young life was so different from that of many other young Iranians. Contrasting with the annihilation of the youths, the bottom third of the page features Marjane attending her first party in a "punk" outfit that her mother made. This contrast becomes visually represented on the page by featuring both versions of Iranian childhood simultaneously, allowing the reader to see the contrast by merely shifting their glance up or down.

The equivalent of this image occurs in the film just after the sequence where Marjane buys outlawed music. While Marjane head-bangs, the image fades out and the music continues. A battlefield appears, and we see portions of a conflict played out to the sounds of Iron Maiden. This music eventually disappears too, and a somber pause occurs before a group of unarmed men charge onto the field and are slowly blown up until only one remains. Finally, he too is killed, and at this moment the background fades to black, leaving only a small remnant of a jagged white explosion over the man's silhouetted body. This too fades to black, and then a key is thrown across the darkness. Here we see the subtlety of the comic's composition, which contrasts two versions of Iranian childhood, eschewed for a more visceral, emotional, and extended battle sequence. In the comic, the revolution and war between Iraq and Iran are rarely given more than a single large panel per instance. Most interesting is the pause on the dying soldier, his death being emphasized for several moments after an extremely visceral battle sequence. Here, lack of motion invites contemplation in a similar way to the comic's use of a large panel to break the flow of the storytelling and invite further investigation of the panel.

The depiction of time is also important to this contemplation. By stretching time to a standstill, the film focuses the viewer on a single aspect, similar to the way the break in panel size focuses the viewer on the entirety of the page. The manipulation of time and how the viewer or reader experiences it helps to control the experience, allowing a complex interaction with the material to take place. The specific construction of time produces different desired outcomes; the comic prefers a slightly more intellectual comparison of the two panels on the page while the film uses this image to emotionally prime the viewer for the scene that will follow. The images are fairly similar and easily comparable even if they are not identical, and while their ultimate purpose is unique to each version of the story, they still function similarly on some levels. It is hard to look at either image and remain cold to the fact that young children are being sacrificed in a conflict that is ultimately meaningless. In the end, the reason each image succeeds in prompting this contemplation is that they understand how their respective media tell stories. The comic shows an understanding that panels and their construction create a basic flow that can be interrupted through manipulating the size, or other aspects, of the panel's overall shape. Similarly the film shows an understanding that motion is a defining aspect of its medium and that removing it, even for only a few moments, will alert the viewer to a change in the story, invite them to ask themselves why this change has occurred, and then allow them to further engage with what they are seeing.

Both versions of *Persepolis* showcase a mastery of the medium that they are working within. An understanding of storytelling norms in both media is what I believe causes these numerous alterations during the process of adaptation. While both media are indeed visual arts and share many storytelling features, these coinciding tools are rarely deployed at the same time or in the same way. Satrapi and her collaborator, Paronnaud, shift and mold the original *Persepolis* into a story that fits perfectly within the world of film and do it by reinventing much of the way that the story is told from an aesthetic standpoint. There is a large resemblance between the two works. The general visual design remains constant and the story is left largely untouched, even if it is abridged. In the end, the changes arrest the attention more than the similarities; it is hard to see the two works as identical pieces rather than two unique and excellent versions of a single story shaped irrevocably by the media in which they are presented.

Why Adapt
Watchmen?

In the fall of 1986, Alan Moore and Dave Gibbons created a groundbreaking work of art that re-examined the context and subtext of super-hero stories. In doing so they completely reinvented the kind of tales that were being told in mainstream comics. *Watchmen* was a watershed moment for the super-hero genre, which means that any adaptation is going to have some lofty expectations attached to it. Zack Snyder's adaptation was never going to be a work of groundbreaking cinematic genius on the level of something like *Citizen Kane,* but Snyder's version of *Watchmen* never comes alive on its own. It certainly animates characters and static images from the comic book, but it doesn't do much more than this. The obsession with recreating the original work ultimately undermines the film. Story beats that work on the printed page don't always translate to a live action story and Snyder is unable to distance himself from the source material long enough to ask himself if portions of the book truly retain their significance when they're brought to life by actors, surrounded by a full score, flashy CGI, and copious amounts of slow-motion photography. All that, along with the concessions Snyder had to make to turn the story into a big budget Hollywood film, hamstrings *Watchmen* from developing its own identity as a film and leaves behind a poor simulacrum of the source material.

That's not to say that everything in the film version of *Watchmen* is overtly beholden to the source material. Its best moments come when it departs from the original piece and carves out its own identity. The best scene of the entire movie is invented. The title sequence is a potent evocation of the history of the *Watchmen* universe and it beautifully lays out decades of exposition in a stylish mix of tableaux-like shots and small moments that inform viewers about the history of super-heroes and how they've altered this version of the world. It's a fantastically crafted sequence that has more verve and wit than anything else in the film. As Bob Dylan sings "The Times They Are a-Changin'" over the slow march of history toward the nuclear apocalypse hanging over the rest of the story, it's hard not to get swept away. The sequence manages to evoke the feel of a comic at times while still utilizing motion. It's a problem that Snyder tries to solve elsewhere in the film by relying on awkward movements, which highlight the comic book's styled poses, and far too much slow motion. Those techniques don't emulate comic panels, though, since they're part of the ongoing progression of the film. Instead they read as modulations of motion rather than the moments out of time that a comic panel represents. The opening titles do, however, evoke the aesthetic of moments out of time. The series of related images that aren't part of the narrative accomplish this. The credits open with the original Night Owl in the act of punching a gun-toting, domino-masked villain in the face. The camera slowly tracks back on this shot as the thug's gun fires in ultra-slow motion. The effect creates the feeling that we're not seeing the entirety of this fight, but merely this one moment, staged to represent the whole of this character's experience fighting crime. It's a moment which, like a comic panel, depicts one distinct action.

That's one of the things this title sequence manages to do so well; it picks and chooses a variety of images that illustrate the ways that the world has reacted to super-heroes, and the kinds of lives those heroes have led. Whether it's the glamorous photo shoot of the original super-hero super-group, The Minutemen, or a bomber flying off to war bearing the image of Sally Jupiter, the original Silk Spectre, the titles gracefully and poignantly tell the story of the first age of super-heroes and the ways in which the second generation of heroes fell to the paranoia and suspicions of their age. *Watchmen* posits a version of the 1980s where Nixon has extended his presidency to what seems like an indefinite term and the threat of nuclear holocaust seems increasingly likely, even with the walking nuclear deterrent, Dr. Manhattan, aligning with US interests. (He is also the only metahuman starring in *Watchmen*.) As the titles progress, fear and dread are introduced throughout the idealized, mostly static, images that make up the early portions of the sequence. A hero is found dead in the revolving doors of a bank. A pair of lesbian lovers is found murdered in bed with the words "lesbian whores" scrawled in their own blood on the wall above them. Sally Jupiter argues with her husband over something indeterminate, and the Comedian is revealed as the true killer of JFK. Conclusively, the title sequence shows how the world was molded by the activity of super-heroes in contemporary history. It's the story in microcosm, and it ends, suitably, in a mini-apocalypse as a crowd protesting vigilantes firebombs a shop window. The ensuing flames blast out over the crowd, consuming them in an echo of the explosion that is the culmination of Adrian Veidt's master plan and the driving force of *Watchmen*'s narrative.

Overall, the title sequence is well equipped to access the super-hero myth, but the scene that precedes it comes nowhere near to matching its ingenuity or effectiveness, which features the death of the Comedian, a nihilistic super-hero contracted by the government for covert wet-work and off-the-books operations, at the hands of Ozymandias, super-industrialist and retired super-hero Adrian Veidt. Veidt is not initially revealed as the killer, but the film is rather direct in implying that Veidt is either the perpetrator or the mastermind behind the Comedian's death.

As Veidt breaks down the Comedian's door there's a commercial playing for a perfume that Veidt manufactures named "Nostalgia." It's part of the scene for a few reasons. First, it allows Snyder to score the forthcoming fight sequence to the song, "Unforgettable" (the first of many painfully on-the-nose sound cues Snyder deploys). The second reason is that the comic features this perfume, as well as a commercial, with the song deployed by Snyder as part of the film narrative. The inclusion is likely an easter egg for fans of the comic who will be able to spot something familiar from the book. Lastly, there is no doubt that the foreshadowing of Veidt being implicated in the murder is meant to create narrative tension throughout the film. The problem, however, with this scene is that it transforms a sequence of dialogue in the comic into a full-fledged brawl. The version of this scene in the comic is interspersed with a pair of detectives coming upon the crime scene and narrating over insert shots of the Comedian being beaten to death. The most important thing to note is that the comic's iteration of the Comedian doesn't throw a single punch. The detectives note

In the comics, the Comedian's final fight occurs in a talky flashback, without him throwing a single punch. From *Watchmen* #1 (Sept 1986). Art by Dave Gibbons. Copyright © DC Comics.

that, "He would have put up some kind of fight I'm certain."[1] But it's hard to take them at their word as they also conclude that it must have taken two men to lift a man as large as Edward Blake (the Comedian's civilian identity). The reason we don't see the Comedian throw any punches in this sequence is that at this point in the story he's been emotionally broken by uncovering Adrian Veidt's plan. It's a plan so cruel, so unfeeling, that even a man who saw life as nothing but one sick joke can't process the enormity of it. He's not going to put up a fight because what he's seen has taken the fight out of him. By removing any resistance from him, Moore and Gibbons project these intentions without giving the Comedian a single line of dialogue.

Snyder does try to convey that the Comedian knew his death was inevitable. Blake utters the line "Just a matter of time I suppose" as his door is broken in and he sees his assailant.[2] The problem lies in the following fight. It's far too intense and is extended to represent the final moments of the wearied Comedian. He fights tooth and nail for survival, and while Veidt dominates the Comedian, the fight does not convey the narrative undertones that imply the Comedian has surrendered. The fight is just an explicit concession Snyder made for the sake of his movie. The comic masterfully utilizes narrative structure to interweave the past and present, presenting the frozen images in time as recreations of dialogue that's spoken in the present. While a film is capable of capturing this style of narrative exposition, it would be moody, and less cinematic. Snyder's version of the sequence sacrifices Moore's character development and replaces it with energized spectacle. Snyder also fails to contextualize the fight as one that is within the scope of average human ability. In the film, the fight depicts two super humans with unbreakable bodies pounding away at one another. The pair punch through concrete walls, throw bodies across the room, and catch knives in mid-air. That's not a problem with most super-hero stories. Certainly, Bruce Wayne can take an inhuman amount of abuse, but the entire purpose of *Watchmen* is to exploit the fragile humanity of super-heroes to test their psychological durability. When the adaptation of a drama opens with a fight sequence, it undermines the mood and severs the intended human connection; the fact that the fight scene doesn't linger on in the comic, but is laboriously re-contextualized in Snyder's film, indicates

[1] Moore, Alan and David Gibbons. *Watchmen*. New York, NY: DC Comics, 2005. Chapter 1, Page 2.
[2] Snyder, Zack. *Watchmen*. Blu-Ray. 2009.

compromise. It all feels off-kilter; it's an extrapolation of material that exists in the book, but it feels focused on getting across thrills rather than replicating the actual intent of the content in its original form.

The most egregious part of the scene is the pairing of the brutal fight with Nat King Cole's "Unforgettable." I already mentioned that it's the first in a long line of song choices that conflict with the tone of the source material. Here, its main purpose is to allow Snyder to "wink" at the audience, juxtaposing a savage fight with a classy, restrained melody. It's a song choice with no subtlety, and it adds nothing to the scene aside from the obvious subtext that the Comedian can't forget what he's seen. It provides an "unconventional" soundtrack to a fight sequence and acts as a too-overt nod to fans of the original comic. It's all flash, meant to highlight just how cool what we're seeing is meant to be. This makes the spectacle of the fight the focus of the scene rather than what the fight means or how it relates to the story. Adding the song makes the fight scene more austere, but unlike the comic's small glimpses of the fight (which are stark and terrifying), Snyder's scoring and stylistic choices make the fight alluring and polished.

Snyder consistently expands small portions of the book into sequences like this, which is understandable considering the mode in which the film was constructed. But too often, he fetishizes violence. Dan and Laurie's assault on a prison to free Rorschach, for example, exhibits the spectacle at work in the film rather than in the comic. Where the violence in the comic is depicted in passing (Dan and Laurie each throw a single punch as they talk about Rorschach), in the film it's an inferior and uninvolving version of the hallway sequence from Chanwook Park's 2003 film *Old Boy*. Whereas that sequence in *Old Boy* beautifully shows the brutality and ugliness of violence, this sequence aggrandizes the leverage and efficacy of resorting to force. Snyder has misinterpreted the casual, almost blunt super-heroics of the comic and recast them as high spectacle.

While the comic manages to slide fights gracefully into panels with multiple points to make, Snyder reformulates these fights as the focus of his scenes, bringing the entirety of his cinematic apparatus to bear on them and thrusting them to the forefront rather than layering them in as details and context. Film is a medium that excels at narrowing attention down to specific details, corralling a viewer's attention. Snyder, however, uses that tendency in such a way that runs counter to the original material. Comics prefer to expand the story with a wealth of detail in each and every panel, and are iconic for doing so. *Watchmen* is a story full of accumulated details, and while Snyder packs many of these details into the frame, he tends to draw the viewer's eye to a lesser aspect of the story after he's done so. This fight sequence is just another example of a sequence that's devoid of anything resembling real content, and it speaks to Snyder's predilection for obsessing over the aesthetics of violence so intently that any attempts to comment on its impact or meaning fall by the wayside. That might be passable in just another rote super-hero film, but *Watchmen* is about what the tropes of super-hero stories mean, and part of that is engaging with the rhetoric of violence.

This tendency is seen throughout the film; during the movie's depiction of Dr. Manhattan's origin we see him dealing with some armed mobsters. Manhattan narrates over the scene that the original Nite Owl, Hollis Mason, called the appearance of Dr. Manhattan, "The dawn of the super-hero." Manhattan comments that, "I am not sure if I know what that means." Billy Crudup's dispassionate narration works well, and his benign confusion is further reflected in the scene when he waves his hand and causes two gangsters to explode, showering bystanders in blood. The scene is raw and potent, and undercuts positivist portrayals of super-heroes, but Snyder can't help but push the concept further, cutting to, and resting the camera on, the bloody guts and skeleton of one of the gangsters, now plastered onto the ceiling. In a scene that's trying to contemplate the uncaring violence that Manhattan is capable of, now that he's transcended his origins as a human, the violence is needlessly exalted. The camera lingers on the viscera in slow motion close-up as the skeletal arm of the man swings back and forth, and this occurs only after we've been shown three separate shots of scantily clad women being showered in blood. It's gratuitous and repetitive, and invokes Snyder's fascination with blood and guts. Alan Moore's intended subtext that explores the anesthetized death-dealing Dr. Manhattan apathetically embraces is lost on the viewer as a result. Snyder's film immerses the viewer in the gory details of the world of *Watchmen*, but does so without comment, using the added motion and sound film provides to amp up the gore and violence while leaving behind the crucial human details. What Moore and Gibbons manage to layer into their version of the story by inviting the reader to ponder the violence being presented to them at their own pace is lost, a victim to adaptation.

The comic's unique presentation doesn't shy away from the brutality of the characters and how they are depicted, but the context guides viewers through the moments of bloodshed. The twelfth issue of *Watchmen,* for example, opens with six full pages depicting the aftermath of Adrian Veidt's horrific attack on New York City. It's a sobering scene that stretches for nearly a fifth of the entire final issue's page count. That intense length is part of what gives it so much power, forcing a reader to ponder the horror of Veidt's ultimate plan for peace. The scene's finale hammers home the human aspect of the catastrophe, though, resting on the image of the newsstand retailer and the young boy's corpses, entwined on the ground in a final embrace. They have been used throughout the comic as a Greek chorus, and clarify the significance of the issue's title, "A Stronger Loving World." This cruel juxtaposition is meant to showcase just how far Veidt is willing to go in his pursuit of what he sees as the salvation of humanity. It's the longest extended sequence of non-dialogue images in the entirety of the comic. The fact that Moore and Gibbons devote that sequence to a meditation on violence and its role in building stability in a world of chaos supports *Watchmen*'s complex relationship with death and destruction – and when it can be justified (or not). It's also cannily constructed to take advantage of the comic-book form—Moore and Gibbons know that to truly engage a reader with the violence, they have to extend their portrayal of it—to the point where even if a reader wants to move past it quickly, they'll have to turn to the next page three separate times to escape it. This makes the violence spatially difficult for the reader to extricate themselves from, especially in a comic that has conditioned readers to look deep into every panel to absorb the minutiae of the world. A film is similar because an image on screen will last for as long as a director decides to keep it there, forcing viewers to confront an image they might not wish to confront. A comic's pacing, however, is also largely a contract between the authors and the readers. Creating a sequence where a reader will willingly wallow in gory, unpleasant details requires careful planning and a mastery of narrative pacing. Nevertheless, Snyder's adaptation does not encroach upon this lurid scene of devastation. His version of the aftermath of the attack never contextualizes the suffering of any particular character, or seeks understanding of brutality in spite of humanism or predispositions to antagonism. Snyder excises the entirety of the six pages leading up to Dr. Manhattan and Laurie's dialogue scene that immediately follows the overview of New York City's destruction in the comic.

Snyder's visuals go for scale rather than human detail in his depiction of the decimated city and showcase the rubble of New York City rather than the human death toll that Moore and Gibbons foreground in their extended sequence. Due to the limited running time that a film imposed on the story, Snyder was unable to develop the characters on the fringe of the story as effectively, so it's not unfair to say that lingering on the human bodies might mean less than it does at times in the comic where those characters had participated in the drama of the larger story as a whole. Rather than decreasing his depiction of the carnage, Snyder completely shies away from violence during the one moment where it is most appropriate to the story, relying on a few brief moments prior to the blast to build the character of those caught in it and then completely eschewing them after the explosion in favor of eulogizing rubble. It's a distinctly impersonal climax to the story and one that speaks to just how poorly Snyder's version of *Watchmen* has built up the world in which the film takes place. Moore and Gibbons' version of the scene evokes the violence that has occurred without fetishizing it, and Snyder routinely has trouble walking that fine line, a line which is so important to the core of this story.

Whether it's the violence, the stylization, or the choice of music, Snyder's credo almost always seems to be "bigger is better," and he never passes up an opportunity to use a sledgehammer to drive a point home, whether it's choosing to score a protest against vigilantes to the tunes of KC and the Sunshine Band's "I'm Your Boogie Man" while Nite Owl and the Comedian hover above like boogeymen, or dropping a muzak cover of Tears for Fears's "Everybody Wants to Rule the World" in an elevator with Veidt. Among the most grating choices in the film is its soundtrack; the most laughable music choice emerges later in the film as Dan and Laurie finally consummate their growing attraction after engaging in some super-heroics. It's a sequence that's meant to be a little strange, both in the comic and the film, but where the comic contents itself with representing the pair's climax through an errant press of a flamethrower button and Nite Owl's ship shooting a pillar of flame into the sky (a moment the film replicates), Snyder takes the scene to new heights of camp. He scores it to Leonard Cohen's original recording of "Hallelujah," a song that's steeped in 1980s synths and one which only grows more campy and unbelievable during the nearly two minute long scene featuring multiple sexual positions, loving close ups of latex booted legs, and some exceedingly graphic thrusting. Snyder intended for the sequence to have a heightened, off-putting feel. He even said in an interview:

> Well, I originally had a different version of "Hallelujah" on that scene— it was the version by Alison Krauss, and it was really beautiful. Too beautiful, as it turned out, because when I showed it to my buddies, they were like, "Wow, you really *mean* this, this love scene." So I was like, okay, that didn't work. But with the Leonard Cohen, in that moment, it's a little sadder of a song, it's a little bit more twisted, it's a little more broken, which expresses to me what's going on in that scene, between those two characters.[3]

He's right that the song makes the sex scene far less beautiful, but when the music is combined with all the other elements Snyder has placed in the scene, it uncomfortably exceeds the concept. Snyder understands the point of the original scene, but his execution lacks the willingness to let the audience come to its own conclusions about the material. The comic doesn't linger as extensively on this scene, and it doesn't feature a score or any of the borderline exploitative cinematography that Snyder employs. By layering in so many new elements over the base content of the comic, he drowns the material in the added storytelling techniques that film provides. Snyder's approach is additive, and the film crumbles under the weight of his direction.

Snyder's directorial enhancements, doing more and adding more into *Watchmen,* play a large part in what sinks the adaptation. He takes the source material and throws it onto the screen with reckless abandon, convinced that if it was a part of the book then of course it will fit into the movie, especially when gussied up with some flashy camera tricks or overly emphatic songs. His song choices are a prime example. While not all of the music he picks originates from the book, the catalog of cultural reference and period pieces from the amplified Cold War period ultimately hurts the film; undermining the original work by including more and more material.

In the buildup to the film's climax, Snyder chooses to deploy Jimi Hendrix's cover of "All Along the Watchtower" as Nite Owl and Rorschach approach Veidt's frozen fortress in the tundra of the South Pole. It's a sequence that appears in both the comic and the movie, and Snyder seizes on it to inject a little extra content after a talky section spent with Silk Spectre and Dr.

---

[3] Parker, James."Interview: Zack Snyder of *Watchmen*." 2009. thephoenix.com/Boston/Movies/77554-Interview-Zack-Snyder-of-Watchmen/?page=2#TOPCONTENT (accessed 19 Nov 2011).

Manhattan on Mars. Hendrix's song, however, feels too obvious a choice for a variety of reasons. It's an overused song for one—it's hardly an original choice for a period piece—and it's so upbeat that it errs on being facetious in light of the narrative stakes at this point in the film. The real reason why the song is inserted here is that in the comic this scene ends with a quotation lifted from the song, attributed to its writer, Bob Dylan. Despite the lyrics being part of the comic, the song choice feels like a miscalculation. Bob Dylan's version of the song would not have been a better choice, but Hendrix's version obscures the scene's intentions. While the lyrics are part of the original work, in a comic there's no aural component to quoting lyrics. Snyder wanted to reference the original work, and believes that this version of the song pairs effectively with the material he's created, but he's still locked himself into a choice of only one song. In doing so, he's picked a song which is simply not a good fit for the scene. It's a moment that further illuminates the ways that adaptation can be fraught with dangers, whether it's straying too far or sticking too closely (Snyder manages to do a little bit of both in this moment). Snyder preserves the original content of *Watchmen*, but in doing so fails to create a suitable new version of the story, or one that functions as anything more than clumsy homage. The text of *Watchmen* survives into the film, but the undercurrent and subtexts that animated the story are lost.

Since Snyder prefers to go big with his directorial choices, it's worthwhile to compare an action scene that both the comic and the film spend some time on, where Snyder's bombastic style might seem like a more logical choice. While the comic tends to be more spartan in its approach to fight scenes and violence than the film, there are a few occurrences where it spends a longer time with its characters during their moments of violence. One notable sequence is Rorschach's attempted, and ultimately failed, escape from the police. Rorschach is trying to figure out just who is bumping off heroes, and his search leads him to an older, retired super-villain named Moloch, the same character to whom the Comedian drunkenly confessed his despair earlier in the story. The scene opens in both the comic and the film nearly identically, with Rorschach stepping in a puddle of water that's illuminated by a neon sign also reflected in the water. The water crashes and ripples out in the wake of his footsteps. Here the scenes begin to depart ever so slightly. Whereas the film has a steady, consistent lighting design, the comic employs an alternating blast of neon light almost every other panel. It creates a rhythm and a sense of strict construction to the storytelling that is further enforced by the grid structure Moore and Gibbons employ. The entirety of *Watchmen* is built out of a nine-panel grid system. Not every page is broken up into nine distinct panels, but all the panels are variations on that setup, and the gutters simply change to allow for larger images. That rigid construction is further highlighted by the decision to depict the flashing neon light, which leads diamond-like shapes or *x*'s to appear when the page is viewed as a whole. The end effect is that the action always feels controlled, and that's further enhanced in this sequence in the comic by the fact that it concludes with the same image with which it began, the neon sign lighting up the puddle, now at rest once more after Rorschach's capture.

The film substitutes that sense of order for a more chaotic approach; Snyder has a flair for action, and he's not afraid to play to his strengths. Where the comic features Rorschach simply walking into Moloch's apartment building, Snyder has Rorschach find the front door locked. This sends him leaping onto the fire escape outside the building and scaling it. When he careens over the railing, Snyder picks a camera angle at eye level and sends Rorschach hurtling at the viewer. It's a combative, kinetic way to film the scene and it speaks to the ways that Snyder is almost always searching to inject action into the story. This switch isn't any sort of betrayal of the material, however. Much like the changes made in adapting *Sin City*, this is an alteration that works with the change in medium. Film can readily display dynamic movements such as characters swinging themselves up onto a fire escape, and the change takes advantage of this fact. Snyder continues to inject motion into the sequence as it proceeds. When Rorschach reaches Moloch's apartment, he sees Moloch sitting in a chair in his kitchen and begins interrogating him, but before long both the comic and the film reveal that Moloch's dead and sporting a rather nasty looking bullet hole right in the center of his forehead. Both scenes highlight this moment, and they do it in unique ways. Snyder utilizes the tools that film allows him and accents the reveal by allowing Moloch's head to loll backward after Rorschach grabs his shoulder; the soundtrack also kicks in and a few blaring, brassy instruments squeal. Rorschach quickly locates the gun used to kill Moloch and before long the police are on a loudspeaker outside telling him to surrender. The comic, on the other hand, doesn't have the ability to kick the soundtrack up a notch or to depict the physical motion of Moloch's head lolling backward. Instead, Moore and Gibbons fall back on the device they set in motion at the beginning of the scene, the flashing neon light that illuminates every other panel, to isolate the image in the middle of the page. The image is a striking close-up that's bathed in yellows and reds and gives the image of Moloch's lifeless body an extremely arresting quality.

The comic version of the scene slows down a bit here when compared to the film, even if the actions presented are the same. Where the film shows Rorschach whipping his head toward something and leaning down slightly to pick up the gun, the comic features an impassive, completely neutral image of Rorschach immediately after he discovers the dead man. The panel doesn't feature the neon splash since it's immediately after the neon lit panel where we find out Moloch has died, and it features no dialogue or narration of any kind. It is simply a medium close-up of Rorschach that invites the reader to contemplate just what he's thinking and how this discovery has affected him.

One of the most interesting aspects of a comic when compared to a film is that while comic panels may take up the exact same amount of space on a page, they can last for entirely unique amounts of reading time, while a frame of a film will always be projected for a set amount of time. That means that if Snyder wants to inject a moment for reflection into this sequence, he has to string out Rorschach's actions and devote more screen time to them. Moore and Gibbons, by contrast, can present an economical sequence of three panels that are well planned and allow for readers to either blow through them or stop and ponder the ramifications of the images being presented to them. One of the main differences between these two sequences is that Snyder focuses more on kinetic excitement than reflection, and in doing so he undermines his attempts to showcase the ways in which Rorschach is doing real damage to other humans. While Snyder certainly tries to carry that thread of the cost of violence through the film, he is too taken with the violence his characters are meting out to pull back and allow the viewer time to reflect on that concept, something that Moore and Gibbons do quite well.

When the actual fight between Rorschach and the police commences, the differences between the material as presented become even more apparent. Snyder features the SWAT team flowing into the building in a series of slow motion shots that are capped by a set of tight shots on the officers counting down to their breach of the room. It's a sequence that plays off the heightened intensity of Rorschach's mad dash around the apartment to arm himself and the frenetic action to come. Snyder loves intensity, and this holds true whether he's slowing down or speeding up the film. The film pacing changes from rapid

In the comic, Rorschach's battle with the police is far simpler. From *Watchmen* #5 (Jan 1987). Art by Dave Gibbons. Copyright © DC Comics.

movements to a snail's crawl as a three count from the officer in charge takes 14 seconds of screen time. The officers never manage to connect with the door since Rorschach opens it, anticipating the strike and knocking them back on their heels. The comic doesn't feature this moment. Instead, it shows the officers kicking down the door and carefully entering the apartment building while talking about Rorschach and whether or not he's there. The approach takes three panels, and while the first shows us nothing but the officers, the second allows us to catch a glimpse of Rorschach's hands and the tools he's employing, a match and an aerosol spray can. The third panel is another that features the blast of neon light, and Rorschach uses that blast to hide the lighting of his match and further showcase just how in control and careful his character is, even in a situation as far out of control as this one.

The film plays the entrance differently, using the moment when Rorschach opens the door to spring back to regular speed. Rorschach quickly attacks the first officer through the door, sending him flying back into his compatriots and then sets about lighting up a handful of matches to use in his makeshift flamethrower, where the comic features only one, carefully utilized match. Snyder places a minimum of five or six in Rorschach's hand as a dramatic extreme close-up highlights him igniting them as he drags them over the wooden floor of the apartment. This shot then transitions into Rorschach repelling two officers with the flames before focusing on a third officer and setting him completely ablaze. Rorschach then whips the spent can at an officer and fires his grappling hook directly into the officer's chest to finish him off. Then Rorschach steals another officer's machine gun, spins in an arc, and hammers the burning officer in the chest, sending him crashing through the stairwell railing and onto his fellow officers. Rorschach takes off running down the hall while another officer tries and fails to shoot him, and Rorschach then breaks through the second story window and plummets to the ground. From the door opening to the moment Rorschach breaks the glass, the scene lasts only 45 seconds, just three times the length of the three count the officers used prior to breaking into the apartment. It's a flurry of action that's absolutely unrelenting and leaves little time, if any, for reflection. In contrast, the comic uses two full pages to depict this sequence. It's not a massive amount of visual space, but the pacing of the scene and the nine-panel structure of the comic make it feel expansive when compared to Snyder's version of the scene.

The action is presented much more simply in the comic. Whereas Rorschach menaced three officers in the film with his flamethrower, in the comic he lights only one officer on fire before retreating and covering his escape by lighting the staircase on fire behind him. Whereas the assault on the officer with a grappling hook spanned only a few seconds in the movie, it garners three full panels in the comic, both a setup panel, one depicting the action, and a final panel showing the aftermath. The aftermath is what the comic version of this scene excels in depicting and is lost in Snyder's whiz-bang approach to the material. While Snyder barrels ahead, Moore and Gibbons are unafraid to slow down and utilize the storytelling techniques at their disposal to really show the damage that Rorschach is doing. After Rorschach lights the officer on fire, there's an entire panel that's devoted primarily to showing the officer reacting to the flames and desperately trying to put them out, while Rorschach escapes in the background. The comic also cleverly uses the lighting that the fire brings to the scene to bathe the bottom two thirds of the page entirely in reds and yellows, allowing the color scheme that represented the flashing lights to suddenly dominate the entire page rather than simply alternating panels. It's a nice bit of storytelling that kicks off the action sequence by showing how Rorschach's actions hang over the entirety of the scene. This further emphasizes the fact that this is a scene about Rorschach and the effects of his method of fighting. In contrast, the biggest grace note that Snyder ever places on the conflagration that Rorschach starts is the aforementioned moment when the officer is sent flying over a railing and into his back-up. The effects of the grappling hook are also keenly felt in Moore and Gibbons's version of the scene, as the final panel depicting this moment shows both an early casualty of Rorschach's assaults writhing in pain in the background of the image, as well as the grappling hook standing upright in an officer lying on the ground in the foreground, the hook itself still held aloft by his chest. The officer can't even manage coherent words, vocalizing only a series of anguished sounds rendered as "Aahuh. / Aaahhhuhg."[4] The sequence feels more real and impactful because Moore and Gibbons take the time to give distinguishable human voices to the men Rorschach is harming. Snyder loses that chance, however, instead focusing on amping up the violence and stylization in an effort to achieve a wild action beat.

---

[4] Moore, Alan and David Gibbons. *Watchmen*. New York, NY: DC Comics, 2005. Chapter V, Page 27.

The two scenes end after Rorschach has jumped out the window and crashed to the ground, but there's one important distinction left that sums up the differences between Snyder's approach to the material versus Moore and Gibbons's approach. In the comic, Rorschach hits the ground and buckles, his legs damaged in the fall. He's then quickly overwhelmed and taken into custody by the cops. In Snyder's version Rorschach lands, rolls, and is up on his feet in an instant, dealing out more damage to police officers unlucky enough to be in his general vicinity. It's a big fight sequence on the heels of a big fight sequence and it adds nothing except prolonging the violence and providing a little more action. Moore and Gibbons wisely design the previous part of the sequence to contain the action, while this final portion focuses on the pathos of Rorschach's character as he's beaten, stripped of his mask, and dragged off. Highlighting those moments are the ever-flashing neon lights, and the final panel which returns to the beginning of the sequence. This illustrates the way in which the lights keep flashing, the sign stays the same, and while Rorschach's worst nightmare has come true, the world hasn't changed in any appreciable way. The only difference is that Rorschach's fedora now lies abandoned alongside the puddle, another bit of detritus in the world, forgotten and left behind. It's a powerful emotion that Snyder's version of the scene loses in favor of ending on Rorschach's howls for the return of his face. It's a big moment, and Snyder can't help but put an exclamation point at the end of a scene that requires no such punctuation.

Zack Snyder had an unenviable job in adapting *Watchmen*. It's a seminal work and a massive undertaking, but his filmic version of the story implies that his heart was at least in the right place. Ultimately, though, his reverence for the source material and his own tendencies toward directorial excess got the best of him, and while he wasn't entirely a slave to the original text, he still stuck closely to it. Snyder's *Watchmen* is never truly his own. It's Snyder's visual retelling of Moore and Gibbons's *Watchmen*, which leads to a mash up of styles and impulses that never truly gels. The story beats are still there, the film hits most of the same notes and thematic concerns of the material, but Snyder's impulses rob the story of its subtlety and poignancy. It's a reverse alchemy wherein Snyder takes apart a carefully constructed machine full of intricately designed parts and reassembles them elsewhere. While it looks similar on the surface, the gears no longer fit quite right and there's something off-kilter about the way the machine runs. The magic disappears, and all that's left is a husk of the original. It looks like *Watchmen*, but where it really counts, it's not. Had Snyder been more willing to retool the story, focusing more on changing it to take advantage of the medium of film, then perhaps he might have found a way to make this story work on the screen. It's a story, however, that's so tied to the medium of comics that it ultimately seems to be too much to ask of any director, much less of one whose guiding impulse seems to have been "make it bigger, make it louder, make it more *Watchmen*."

Scott Pilgrim Vs. the Adaptation

The *Scott Pilgrim* series of comics is a bold, playful work that frequently and gleefully bounds around the printed page. It's a comic that plays fast and loose with the traditional aesthetics of the medium, pushing the storytelling into a frenzied, anything goes arena where it's hard to tell just what will appear on the next page. It could be a massive fight involving robots and swords sprouting from chest cavities, an actual recipe for vegan shepherd's pie, or a tutorial on how to play a song from the lead character's band. There's simply a lot going on in the book, much of which takes full advantage of the comic-book medium, so an adaptation of Bryan Lee O'Malley's opus was going to be a labor-intensive task for whoever took on the job. Luckily, it ended up in the hands of Edgar Wright, a genre-melding, forward-thinking, mad scientist of a director whose personal style and quirkiness fit beautifully with the material. What is most striking about Wright's adaptation is both how closely it hews to the comic in some regards—huge swaths of the dialogue are lifted directly from it—and how it completely leaves fidelity behind when it's in the best interest of the movie. The aforementioned dialogue is repurposed and emerges from differing characters' mouths regularly. Wright clearly has affection for the source material, but rather than try to make a faithful adaptation of the comic book, he spins off in his own direction. Wright focuses on what makes the comics work, taking what he can and adding what's needed to keep the affair moving forward smoothly. Wright also focuses on an important stylistic element of the comic and repurposes it for the world of film: video games. Both the comic and the film feature a main character whose childish sense of self warps his worldview. Scott Pilgrim sees his life through the lens of video games and that in turn shapes the viewer's perception of the world. Wright takes his cue from this fact and creates a film that revels in the world of video games, adding musical cues ripped directly from game soundtracks, highlighting the comic's boss-battle-inspired structure, and employing a myriad of other tricks to help make the movie come alive both as a distinctively cinematic work of art and as a heavily referential text.

There's another reason to look at this adaptation, though. The *Scott Pilgrim* series of comics was released during the beginning of the cinematic boom of comic properties and the series was optioned before it had finished in print. Edgar Wright was brought on and development of the movie commenced before the comic was finished. When Wright insisted that Bryan Lee O'Malley, the writer/artist behind *Scott Pilgrim*, be involved with the movie, it created a situation where the comics and the film began to feed off one another. As the film neared shooting O'Malley was still working on the books, and since he was involved in the film, aspects of it began to creep into his own work. O'Malley describes this cross-pollination as such:

> They had finished the final shooting draft of the movie before I had started the sixth book. They sort of knew what they were doing, I mean they had my notes for the sixth book, and I kind of incorporated experiences I had during the shoot of the film into the sixth book.[1]

The release dates for the sixth and final volume of the series and the film ended up being less than a month apart, with the comic being released on July 20th 2010 and the film following on August 13th of the same year. Each shared elements, but the unique versions of the story that are being told lead the characters and the narrative to different conclusions. It's reasonable to assume that the co-development of the stories is part of the reason why this happened. The creators of the film were likely only working with O'Malley's description of where his story was headed, but the changes that do arise speak to a deeper division in the works. *Scott Pilgrim vs. the World* is more than just a recreation of O'Malley's *Scott Pilgrim*; it's a different take on the same elements.

---

[1] Winning, Josh. "Q&A: Scott Pilgrim creator Bryan Lee O'Malley." 2010. totalfilm.com/news/q-a-scott-pilgrim-creator-bryan-lee-o-malley/page:4 (accessed 4 Feb 2012).

One of the biggest rifts between the comic and the film is that the comic is simply more expansive. The story is spread over six volumes, which allows it to tread down more narrative alleys while telling Scott's tale. Any film adaptation is subject to narrative limitations and must condense a larger printed work into a more focused one that can fit within a feature film's running time. Wright turns that fact to his advantage, though, focusing on the story's key elements and forging ahead with reckless abandon. While O'Malley's *Scott Pilgrim* wallows in the details of its world at times, Wright's version restructures the story into a tight narrative revolving around Scott Pilgrim's journey into adulthood.

The comics open with three two-page spreads, the first of which is a stark image of Ramona, a character the reader has yet to meet, trudging through snow wrapped in a hefty coat. Her head is down, and the only words on the page are "Oni Press Presents"[2] and Bryan Lee O'Malley's author credit. It's an image that fills most of the page with pure, uninterrupted white, and it's a somber start to a raucous tale. Indeed, it picks up within moments, as the next two-page spread is the title page. It features two Scott Pilgrims, one on each page, rocking out with their bass guitars. The words "Scott Pilgrim"[3] flow out of Scott's basses, the text manifesting through the amplified sound. It's a major contrast to the initial image and the former, serious emotional content. (O'Malley's meshing of divergent moods is one of his artistic signatures, along with the over-the-top aesthetic he brings to the world of the comics.) Wright's opening kicks off in unique form with the Universal logo reimagined as the intro to an 8-bit video game. The Universal title card all film viewers know so well is pixelated, the globe spinning choppily as if some unseen processor can't quite render enough frames to make it spin uninterrupted, and the traditional Universal musical cue is recast in a bleep and bloop filled version of itself. It's pure video game, and it's important to note that rather than play up the fact that *Scott Pilgrim vs. the World* is a comic-book adaptation, Wright has instead chosen to foreground the video-game influences that shaped the comic and will similarly inform the movie. O'Malley also utilized a similar homage to video games in a title for the comic, but it would only come in the fourth volume

---

[2] O'Malley, Bryan Lee. *Scott Pilgrim's Precious Little Life*. Portland, OR: Oni Press, 2004. Page 1.
[3] Ibid, pages 3-4.

when he placed Scott and Ramona within a winged circle that's a direct homage to the *Sonic the Hedgehog* series of video games.

The film quickly takes this video game homage even further. The film and comic both open with an exterior shot of Stephen Stills and Young Neil's home. The comic deploys this establishing shot as the final two page spread before the comic proper starts, and fills the left page with the legal front matter and publishing credits. The right page shows mostly the snowy air above a row of houses and features a dialogue balloon informing the reader that Scott Pilgrim is, in fact, dating a high schooler. The film flows from the Universal title card onto a similarly grey sky. In fact, the grey sky is actually created when the Universal logo flies at the viewer and the "E" in the logo becomes the sky. Some supertitles then appear on the screen and a narrator reads them, informing us that the story takes place in Toronto, Canada in the not-so-distant past, and that, yes, Scott Pilgrim is dating a high schooler. It's roughly the same information the comic relates, but it's also more specific in that it gives an exact location to the story. In general, the film prefers clarity and directness in comparison to the comic, since it has a large portion of content to cover in approximately 2 hours of run time. After the narration has been delivered, the image begins to tilt down toward the ground, and accompanying this tilt is yet another musical infusion of video game music. The music recalls the score from the *The Legend of Zelda* series of video games, and that homage carries over into the next scene as Young Neil, Nintendo DS in hand, plays an unseen video game that highlights and punctuates the scene with aural cues that any fan of the *Zelda* series will instantly recognize. As the scene progresses and Scott reveals more and more about his mysterious new girlfriend, he states that she's Chinese. In the film, this is accompanied by a sound effect from the *Zelda* series that plays whenever some sort of mystery has been revealed. It's yet another clever addition from Wright that speaks to the ways that Scott views his life as a video game. O'Malley also punctuates this moment in the comic; when Scott says "Chinese" the word itself appears bolded, indicating the way he's stressing the revelation to his friends. The comic might have discovered some way to tie this reveal into a video-game-fueled motif, but it's a fairly minor one. As the comic has yet to reveal the depth of its video-game inspiration, it would be an odd choice to deploy so early. The film is able to use the far less obtrusive sound design to start to show the ways that video games will influence its stylistic choices while driving ahead the story. Both communicate the same information. Wright simply seizes upon an opportunity that is afforded to him thanks to one of the filmic tools at his disposal.

The final double-page spread before the first Scott Pilgrim volume, *Scott Pilgrim's Precious Little Life* (July 2004), begins. Art by Bryan Lee O'Malley. Copyright © Bryan Lee O'Malley.

Another trait that both versions of *Scott Pilgrim* share is that they're extremely kinetic works. Both O'Malley and Wright invest the work with real vigor; the story bounces from scene to scene and style to style erratically. It's not surprising that a film could invest this kind of story with that kind of kineticism through its many uses of motion, and Wright is indeed a director with a penchant for tools such as snap zooms and quickly whipping cameras. The fact that the comic also manages to create a quick-moving story that seems to pull the reader along without regard for their desires is all the more impressive. Comics have a much harder time delineating the passage of time than film, and where a film can choose exactly how long a given action or motion will take, in a comic it's up to the reader to decide how long they'll look at any one image. Paradoxically, one of the ways that the *Scott Pilgrim* comics manage to create the feeling of an accelerated pace is by packing pages with an abundance of visual information. O'Malley doesn't always utilize this technique, but he's not afraid to overload the page with a plethora of things to notice. By giving the reader many potential focus points, O'Malley creates an atmosphere where a reader begins to feel like they have to rush to take in everything. Panels are filled with information to digest which fosters a desire in the reader to scan forward and catch back up with the narrative, propelling them through the story at a faster rate. Whereas many images without any sort of text can invite a reader to slow down and ponder the artwork on display, a more densely packed panel can lead to readers speeding up in an attempt to keep pace with the story being told.

Early in both the film and the first volume of the comic, Knives Chau sits in on band practice and is quickly awed by Scott's band, Sex Bob-Omb. Both Wright and O'Malley craft sequences that take advantage of the tools at their disposal, but each creates an overwhelming set of images which establish a tone for the story moving forward. Both the comic and the film count into the song in roughly the same way as Kim announces, "We are Sex Bob-Omb! / One Two Three Four!"[4] The comic then transitions into a two-page spread with four panels along the top of the image and five along the bottom. The bulk of the page is taken up by an image of Sex Bob-Omb playing. The top images feature a slow push in on Knives's increasingly starry eyes as she is transfixed by the band's music, and the bottom stretch of images are extreme close ups of things like Stephen Still's singing mouth or Kim's foot kicking the bass drum pedal on her drum kit. That's not all the two-page spread does, though. It also features a how-to guide for those who want to learn how to play the actual song. In the upper left of the panel featuring Sex Bob-Omb playing, there's a small caption box featuring the chords required to play the song which are then paired with lyrics that flank the stretch of panels along both the top and bottom of the image. It's a dense array of information that speaks to what separates comics from film. A film could certainly put all this information onto the screen, but it would be extremely difficult for the viewer to take it all in, whereas on the printed page, the lyrics and chords provided can be revisited if a reader so desires. In the filmic version, a viewer would have to wait until he or she had a personal copy of the film and then be stuck skipping backward and forward to get at this information. Part of what makes this stylistic quirk in the comic so enjoyable is the knowledge that it's a functional set of instructions that could actually be utilized. In a film the hurdles to actually using the information would

---

[4] Ibid, page 18.

be much greater and would likely make its inclusion feel more like a silly gimmick than it does in the comic, even if it is a very whimsical addition to the scene. O'Malley is never afraid of getting ridiculous, though, and this inclusion of a fully fleshed out how-to guide on a song is one of the first big hints that the comic is more than willing to try some very, very strange things, and it works wonderfully.

Bryan Lee O'Malley details instructions on how to play the song featured in the story, along with the song's full lyrics. From *Scott Pilgrim's Precious Little Life* (July 2004). Art by Bryan Lee O'Malley. Copyright © Bryan Lee O'Malley.

The film also features a version of this sequence. Instead, as the band starts to play, the camera begins to track back from the band and eventually the living room has become impossibly elongated. The shot settles on Knives Chau and Young Neil sitting on the couch, with Knives's utter astonishment at the band's talent, represented by the aforementioned surreal nature of the suddenly elongated living room. As the band plays, stylized lightning bolts undulate around their bodies, evoking both the comic-book heritage of the story and standing in as a physical representation of the music being played. Finally the words "Scott Pilgrim" explode forward from the band and the camera cranes down behind the couch as the rest of the film's title meets up with the descending "Scott Pilgrim." The title bursts apart and the film segues into its title sequence: an animated, motion-filled homage to the abstract films of directors like Stan Brakhage. The title sequence features a bevy of images that foreshadow the story of the film to come. Most of the characters and events are represented in one way or another by images that spastically drift around the frame as if they were imprinted on celluloid that doesn't quite match up from one frame to the next. As a sequence, it's a sugar rush of sounds, images, and ideas. Much like O'Malley's method of putting massive amounts of information in front of the reader to overload their senses, Wright assaults the viewer with music and rapidly shifting images to approximate the utter bewilderment that Knives Chau feels in the moment. The sequence also serves as an introduction to just how over the top the film can be. Sure, the movie opens with stylized narration and an 8-bit soundtrack, but here Wright makes a point of showing how he's going to push the film in a variety of directions rather than be content with making a movie infused with video-game or comic-book tropes. In the same spirit as O'Malley's books, which struggled to find any strange concept they didn't want to include, Wright's open to pushing his version of *Scott Pilgrim* anywhere that the medium of film will allow him to push it.

As the abstracted images fade away and reality (or at least what passes for reality in the Scott Pilgrim universe) reasserts itself, Wright returns to images of the band. Much as in the final panels of O'Malley's two-page spread Wright settles on tight shots of the band as they're playing. He adds one important component to these shots, though: motion. The camera wildly swings along with the characters as they play, while editors Jonathan Amos and Paul Machliss intersperse quick shots of Knives Chau featuring a slow zoom in. It's a condensing of the images that lined the two-page spread. Whereas in the comic those sets of images took up two separate areas of the page, in the film they can be more effectively merged. In a comic it would be difficult to intersperse these images because the slow zoom that O'Malley takes four panels to build would likely read less effectively if each portion of the zoom were offset by an unrelated image. The zoom is apparent in the comic because the previous image is still visible as one moves on to the next panel. If there were other images breaking up that slow zoom, it would be harder for the reader to parse as a continuous move-in on a character. Film has no such problem, particularly because of the contrasting speeds that Wright uses to compare the energy of the band shots with the subtler zoom that's characterizing Knives. In fact, by cutting between shots featuring a manic, unrestrained energy and shots that have a focused, low-key feeling, Wright amplifies the effect of the slow zoom. Film is able to compare these two motions in a way that comics cannot, so Wright takes advantage of that fact to help highlight just how blown away Knives is by her new boyfriend's band, while O'Malley wisely structures his comic in a way that allows him to convey the same information without confusing the reader. Both methods work quite well, and both are perfectly appropriate to their medium. O'Malley's version separates out two different storytelling techniques for clarity; the upper panels that zoom in on Knives feature a tighter, more traditionally narrative-oriented sequence while the bottom images are loose and unrelated without any real sense of narrative flow. Wright, on the other hand, highlights the ways that film can present rapidly switching, dissimilar images while still creating a comprehensible procession of events. It's a short sequence in both the comics and the film, but either version of it speaks to what the reader or viewer should expect from the story to come and what kinds of techniques will be used to tell it.

Wright and O'Malley both employ an aggressive, heavily stylized aesthetic, and there are few better places to further dig into those aesthetics than during the fight sequences that help structure the story of *Scott Pilgrim* in both the comics and the film. The fights ultimately dictate the story to a degree, as Scott must defeat Ramona's seven evil exes if he wants to be with her. The first of these fights is between Scott and Matthew Patel, and it takes place during a performance by Sex Bob-Omb. This fight sequence actually expands on the material in the comic, or at least lets it breathe more, as opposed to being truncated for a film's shorter run time. The film has quite a few moments where the physical act of fighting becomes the focus of the scene, while the comic rarely lets a panel go by without adding some sort of dialogue or exposition. Much of the information both the film and the comic communicate is the same, but whereas the comic keeps the fight going in nearly every panel, even if exposition or dialogue is also taking place alongside the action, the film is more willing to slow down so as to contrast the frantic moments where punches and fireballs are flying with slower pieces of the confrontation, where only words are being exchanged. This is apparent in the way that the works handle the transition from Sex Bob-Omb playing to Matthew and Scott fighting. The comic features only the briefest moment of the band playing; Stephen Stills gets out just three words before Patel comes crashing through The Rockit's ceiling. The film, in contrast, spends over a minute on the band in their set. During this time, Wright fills that screen time with a variety of shots and camera moves that highlight and build on the character relationships that have been growing over the course of the film. It's a deft sequence that gets in a few solid jokes, focuses in on Ramona's growing attraction to Scott, and lets the movie take advantage of the song that's been composed for the occasion. The comic has certainly proven at this point that it can build a sequence around a band playing a song, but O'Malley decides against portraying it here. Part of the decision may relate to the fact that an extended song sequence here would likely not be that interesting on the page. The advantage of having actual audio in a film is that the aural quality of the song itself can be enough to distinguish one music sequence from another. A comic, however, needs to find a visual style to represent that sound. The comic achieves this with the band Crash and the Boys, whose brand of music is so assaultive that it is represented by a two page spread sporting only jagged bolts of lighting, some brief lyrics, and a sprinkling of black dots at the center of the image. The comic could certainly find a new way to showcase Sex Bob-Omb playing, but O'Malley decides against it as he's just included a musical interlude of sorts. Much like the rest of the sequence, O'Malley chooses to forge ahead, focusing on the most essential parts of the scene being presented. Wright chooses to paint more broadly, though, and he's able to do this because whereas expanding a comic scene to encompass more characters takes up more time and page real estate, a film has an easier job of cutting between stories and characters. Cutting to a character in the middle of a song or fight can take only a second or two in a film, but in a comic it requires a full panel to be drawn and fit onto a page. While a six volume series of comics can explore more narrative avenues over its page count, a two-hour film is more readily able to explore the scenes that make up its running time. Wright squeezes every ounce of tension and comedy that he can out of the characters and relationships that he's established and he does so by using the flexibility that film editing allows.

While both works utilize their medium in unique ways, they are still bound by some of the same basic storytelling needs. In the moments before Matthew Patel flies through the ceiling of the club, both the film and the comic foreshadow this event in unique ways. The comic does so by presenting Matthew's intrusion in a two-page spread where the bulk of the right side of the page is given over to his careening flight into the Rockit. The left side of the page is filled with panels that depict Sex Bob-Omb starting to play, being interrupted by a crash sound effect, and then three individual panels of Scott, Stephen, and Kim reacting to the sight of a human being hurtling through a ceiling. O'Malley is ingeniously making use of the way readers experience comics. Since a reader is guaranteed to notice the huge image of Patel flying through the air the second they turn the page, they're always aware that Sex Bob-Omb's song is going to be interrupted. It's simply impossible not to see Patel, and as the reader continues down the page, the panels leading into the big splash of Patel take on a less rigidly defined sense of narrative progression. A reader is still led through the page, but by the time they've reached the bottom three panels that each feature one member of Sex Bob-Omb, those panels no longer feel like one event that is coming after another; they're images of the people all reacting to Patel's appearance at once. Readers of comics consume pages in a holistic fashion, even when they're presented with a straightforward reading order that conforms to the traditional left-to-right, top-to-bottom structure of comics.

Matthew Patel arrives on the scene in *Scott Pilgrim's Precious Little Life* (July 2004). Art by Bryan Lee O'Malley. Copyright © Bryan Lee O'Malley.

Wright also feels compelled to highlight the forthcoming shift in the scene from Sex Bob-Omb playing to Scott and Patel fighting, but he is unable to manipulate time in the same way that the comic can. Instead Wright relies on a pair of stylistic tricks to get the job done. As the moment nears, the film features a shot that begins with Kim Pine alone on the left third of the screen. As she continues to play, Scott suddenly appears in his own panel of sorts, in the middle third of the screen. Finally Stephen Stills receives his own third of the image on screen right. It's a shot that's quite similar to the three panels of the characters in the comic in the way that it portrays them in distinct areas, but gives them temporal unity at the same time. It also highlights a pronounced stylistic shift in the scene as the rest of the musical number has lacked any sort of overt stylization. Most of the shots feature slow, restrained camera movement and there's also a lack of rapid cutting during this sequence. It's not a scene that overwhelms the viewer like many others in the film; it's a slower prelude to the upcoming explosive fight.

The first hint of the battle to come is the switch from a lack of overt stylization to the eclectic three panel shot that emerges. The film also highlights Patel's presence with a subtle audio cue. As the three panel shot nears its end, a soft but distinct bit of sound modulation comes into play, giving the song an added effect that is akin to feedback from an amp. It's a short effect, lasting for no more than two seconds, but between this and the unique shot choice, it hints at Patel's appearance and the shift in the scene that is about to occur. The difference between the comic and the film is that the comic is able to quite literally use its future to comment on its present, whereas a film is only able to foreshadow its future with its present. Since a comic isn't constrained by time in the same way that film is, it can utilize different techniques to build its story and comment on what is happening; however, it also forfeits some of the benefits that come from having a distinct and regimented relationship with time.

The film and the comic also use differing techniques to highlight the shift in narrative that results from the outbreak of the fight between Scott and Patel. Both use more than a few tricks to get the job done; the film once again highlights motion and action while the comic uses the fluidity of its construction to great effect. In the film, Patel's attack, from the declaration of his intent to battle Scott to the first blow being struck, takes 16 full seconds. Wright accomplishes this by slowing the action to a crawl and lingering on Scott's confusion over just what is happening. In slow motion shots, Scott repeatedly asks rhetorically, what he should do. It's only when Wallace Wells screams out "Fight" that he finally snaps into action, unplugging his bass, throwing it to Young Neil, and stepping into a fighting stance. The film punctuates this shift by throwing in a bevy of stylistic flourishes. Wallace's words echo over the next few shots, adding to the strange heightened nature of the scene: the lights behind Patel shift out of focus and grow larger and less concretely defined, a display appears behind Scott (complete with video-game sound effects that proclaim "Fight!") and encircles Scott in a player indicator, and the aspect ratio of the film shifts, moving from the film's standard 1.85:1 ratio to the wider 2.35:1. All of this tells the viewer that he or she is in for a sequence that's going to push the already heightened reality of the Scott Pilgrim universe one step further. The comic doesn't utilize quite as wide a variety of techniques to showcase this change in the narrative, but it signals it all the same. The shift happens much more quickly in the comic. The moment when Patel appears until the moment when Scott blocks his first punch is covered in only three panels, but O'Malley makes the most of that space. The most impactful change comes from how O'Malley chooses to lay out his pages. Whereas most of the comic is built around panels that feature right angles flush with the edges of the book, the fight sequence is comprised entirely of gutters that cut diagonally across the page, creating layouts that are more fluid and reflective of the kinetic nature of the fight. The other major technique O'Malley uses during the fight is leaving out backgrounds of panels in favor of motion lines that once more serve to highlight the speed and frenetic pace of the fighting. Not every panel is filled with these lines. In moments when the fighting subsides or where we see other characters watching the fight, the regular backgrounds return, but they serve as one further way to tip the viewer off to the change in the scene.

A film could certainly obfuscate the background of a scene. Wright even takes steps in this direction, such as the moment when the background lights flare up and become less obvious aspects of the Rockit's décor and more stylish accents to the characters and their actions. The way O'Malley uses these motion lines is unique to the medium of comics, though, and the prevalence of them would be hard to mimic in a film. Were the film to completely obscure the backgrounds during the shots involving the fight and then have them return during shots not involving the fight, it would likely cause a visual whiplash of sorts as viewers were forced to bounce back and forth between shots that only remain on screen for a few seconds, featuring completely contrasting visual styles. Such an effect can be powerful in the short term, and Wright does choose to abstract the background during Scott's aerial juggle of Patel, but if it were spread out over the entirety of the fight sequence, it would likely become difficult to watch. The comic has no such problem with this issue, though, since whenever it ends up switching to a panel with a normal background, the motion lines are still present in the edge of the reader's eye, giving the page a unity even as it demonstrates subtle shifts in style. Instead of doubling down on a singular effect as O'Malley does, Wright runs the gamut of techniques that film provides him with: he throws CGI constructs into the frame, messes with the aspect ratio, slows and speeds up the film, keeps the camera flowing freely throughout the fight, and throws in a song and dance number for good measure. It's a rapidly changing, reality-breaking fight that's acknowledged as such; Scott's sister, Stacy, is even confused over Patel's sudden shift into song. O'Malley's efforts are more focused, but they're just as effective at showcasing how heightened the fight is. During the fight sequence, the motion lines even end up being used as gutters for panels in certain instances. The effect allows O'Malley to structure the action when necessary but also permits the chaos of the fight to literally break down the structure of the page once the reader has gotten their bearings. The film effectively juggles a variety of styles without totally overwhelming the viewer, while the comic utilizes fewer techniques but pushes them further than the film does with any one of the techniques it uses. Wright playfully uses techniques such as sound design and the free flowing movement of both the actors and the camera to lend an air of unreality to the fight, while O'Malley changes the structure of his page and depiction of the world for the same effect.

The aesthetic of unreality is a key aspect of both the film and the comic as each depicts Scott as a young adult growing into maturity. Part of that journey involves leaving behind his childish, self-centered worldview, and part of that outlook on life is the way in which Scott transforms his world into a fantasy. Scott sees everything through a veneer of pop-culture ephemera, and while part of the joy of the movie and comic is that sheen of insanity, both posit it as a way for Scott to escape from the harsh reality of his life. One of the key techniques for highlighting Scott's shifting between reality and unreality in the comic comes from the way O'Malley colors the gutters between panels. When O'Malley depicts events in the story such as flashbacks or dream sequences, the borders change from the traditional white that typifies the rest of the comic into pure black. It's a simple, easily recognizable shift that would at first seem difficult to replicate in a filmic environment. Wright deploys plenty of split-screen effects and uses borders briefly during those moments, but since those split-screens are never a default mode for the film, it's nearly impossible to create a sense of normalcy that can then be broken by an eventual stylistic deviation. As I noted, early on in the fight between Scott and Patel, a shift in aspect ratio signifies the start of the fight and the transition into the heightened video game aesthetic that dominates it. One of the benefits of this shift from the 1.85:1 ratio to the 2.35:1 ratio is that it adds a pair of black bars to the screens. They're not technically gutters, and since those bars are traditionally black, trying to replicate the standard white gutters would be a non-traditional aesthetic for a film. But they do create an area of the screen that Wright can play with that isn't explicitly tied to the visuals that make up the actual content of the film. It's a trick that most films don't attempt, and it's particularly well-suited to the world of *Scott Pilgrim*.

During this fight sequence, Wright uses the shifting aspect ratios to set up a more drastic use of empty space on screen. Ramona launches into the backstory of her history with Patel in both the comic and the film, and when she does so, the style shifts. In the comic, the first panel of Ramona's story features her against a totally black background as she drapes her arms over the panel below her. It's a neat bit of page layout by O'Malley that depicts the memory we're entering as Ramona's, and the cartoonish, almost crayon-drawn visuals along with the inverted color palette evoke a sense of the past. O'Malley structures the memory more like a storybook than a comic, removing any dialogue bubbles and placing all the narration within the gutters to create a sequence that feels substantially different from the "reality" of the present. Wright also delves into a similar aesthetic; so similar, in fact, that the film transitions into a series of comic panels in O'Malley's style that are nearly identical to the panels in the book. There are differences however, such as the dialogue being altered, the panels receiving touches of color, and, most importantly, added motion. The characters themselves don't truly move, but they do slowly shift position in the image, giving the impression that the characters are acting out the fights and romances being depicted. Most important though is that the panels themselves actually move in and out of frame. Wright opens the sequence with a shot of the real-life Ramona beginning to talk. As she does, the lights behind her fade away and she's left against an utterly black background. The camera then quickly tilts down to a drawn image of Ramona in middle school. The image itself takes up the screen space only partially and leaves large swaths of it unoccupied by anything other than blackness. Wright, like O'Malley, has decided to use black backgrounds to help showcase this stylistic shift into the depiction of a memory, but unlike O'Malley, Wright has to figure out a way to help deploy this aesthetic. By shifting into a fusion of motion comics and film, he allows himself the further leeway of not utilizing the entirety of the screen at every moment. In the same way, the heightened dream states that Scott finds himself in from time to time allow Wright to get away with altering the aspect ratio mid-film. During the sequence, panels fly in from the top, bottom, and sides of the frame. The panels also expand to reveal more information, and overlap one another. It's a sequence of images that wouldn't function as a comic because it's structured to tell its story through still images infused with motion, rather than solely the juxtaposition of images.

Bryan Lee O'Malley uses crayon-like visuals to evoke a sense of the past. From *Scott Pilgrim's Precious Little Life* (July 2004). Art by Bryan Lee O'Malley. Copyright © Bryan Lee O'Malley.

This divide speaks once again to a key difference between comics and film that we've continually returned to: how the two media depict motion. This distinction becomes apparent in one of the alterations made by Wright in the film. His depiction of Ramona's fourth evil ex, Roxy Richter, changes her fighting style and choice of weapons. The film also condenses the fight into a single scene whereas it plays out over multiple scenes in the book. That's likely a concession to the film's running time, though, rather than anything of deeper significance to dissect. The two fights depicted share one thing in common, the first of which is that each features Ramona and Roxy engaging in the battle too, rather than just presenting Scott combatting this ex. The most important change in the film is the fact that Roxy's weapon is different. In the comic, it's a standard katana, but in the film it's a combination of a whip and a sword that Roxy brandishes and lashes out with in a whirlwind of speed and violence. It leads to a quick-moving, visually intoxicating sequence that relishes the sheer kinetic motion of the fight. Ramona flips, turns, dodges, and leaps through the air in an effort to stay one step ahead of Roxy's weapon, which seems to be everywhere at all times. Wright's direction only heightens the sense of swirling motion as his camera twists and flows with the dance of violence he's depicting.

When the scene needs to add Scott into the mix, Wright pushes the battle one step further into a dance battle. Once Ramona has stopped Roxy's initial assault, Roxy points out that Scott is the only one who can truly defeat her if he wants to remain Ramona's boyfriend. Scott is, however, unwilling to hit a girl, which leads to Ramona's taking the lead and guiding Scott through the fight in a sequence that plays on the similarities between dances and fights in film by fusing the two styles into one. Ramona grabs Scott and twirls him into her grasp, sending his fists out to parry, counter, and slap Roxy. It's a remarkably clever and subtle change to the scene and Wright pulls it off with aplomb. It also plays to the strengths of film much in the same way that the alteration of Roxy's sword did. Film has the benefit of being able to portray smaller, subtler motions as well as clearly depicting every instant of every motion that makes up the movie. A film can show every crack and undulation of a whip as well as all the subtle interactions of two characters dancing / fighting with one another, whereas a comic is left to imply almost the entirety of those movements in a scant few images. As Ramona flicks her feet around in quick, assured motions we see the immediate results come to life as Scott's feet suddenly fly into place, shunting away Roxy's blows and Ramona and Scott landing a few shots of their own. It's a sequence that would be hard-pressed to function in the bounds of a comic panel. The subtle variations of motion and the rapid-fire movements would quickly eat up page space and simply be difficult to make legible for a reader. You could show Ramona kicking Scott's feet, but the physicality of the film lets the viewer observe exactly what happens, thanks to each of Ramona's movements, while a comic would have to suggest those effects. Where a film is able to fill in almost all of the blanks, at least in terms of the movements of the characters, a comic has to leave much of that work up to the reader. Getting the information that Ramona is truly guiding the fight wouldn't be impossible in a comic, but it would be unlikely to have the same grace and fluidity that the film is capable of.

Whereas the film decides to pay homage to dance sequences in the fight with Roxy, the comic chooses to evoke another type of filmic standoff in Scott's climactic fight with Ramona's half-ninja ex. O'Malley frames the final battle between the two in the style of samurai showdowns found in classic films like *Seven Samurai*. The two square off and charge at one another, leaping into the air and landing with each combatant seemingly unharmed. Then, suddenly, one betrays that they've lost the battle and the fatal wound they've been dealt becomes apparent. It's an appropriate style of fighting to translate into the comic medium since it relies on extremes of motion rather than subtle movements and changes like a dance sequence requires. It's built around complete stillness and utter speed. Stillness isn't a problem for comics and while a comic can't literally depict rapid motion, it can suggest it easily enough. O'Malley depicts Scott and Roxy charging each other in a two page spread featuring Scott on the left side of the page and Roxy on the right. The images suggest that the two are careening toward the center of the image where the pair will meet. O'Malley implies the speed with which they move by positioning Scott on the left-hand side of a double-page spread, with Roxy on the right. Each page has three panels, mirroring each other and emphasizing the pair's conflict. The second and third of these panels, on both pages, feature motion lines, and the third panel on both pages depicts their respective characters' cropped feet, as they leap into the air – with sound effects added for extra drama. The two pages perfectly express that Scott and Roxy have moved from a standstill to an absolute sprint, and it does so with only a few sparse images and suggestive comics idioms.

Bryan Lee O'Malley borrows tropes from visual narratives associated with ninja action films to stage the battle with Ramona's half-ninja ex. From *Scott Pilgrim Gets it Together* (Oct 2007). Art by Bryan Lee O'Malley. Copyright © Bryan Lee O'Malley.

Comics allow the story, and its motions, to live in the mind of its reader. Part of the reason why the choice of this samurai-inspired battle is so ingenious is that every aspect of it is left up to the viewer's or reader's imagination, whether it takes place in film or on the printed page. In a movie, the viewer sees the moment of the strike, but is left wondering just who won the encounter. It's a moment that exploits an observer's perspective, and it's an example of film taking a similar aesthetic approach to the style of storytelling that a comic grapples with constantly. When Scott and Roxy attack one another, it's in a large splash panel that takes up the majority of the two pages, and because it's a comic, absolutely every moment of that single blow is left up to the reader. Though a film has to show the slash of the blade, the comic need only present the two figures, side by side against the moon in the sky with their blades out. It's an image that allows the reader to ponder the fight and wonder about just what they've missed, and it fits beautifully in a comic because every panel leaves so much unsaid. When the pair land and it begins to become apparent that Scott has won, O'Malley continues to translate the aesthetics of old samurai films into comic-book terms. Roxy admits defeat, and much like in those old films a wound suddenly becomes apparent on her body, a slash that cuts cleanly through her body. O'Malley cleverly utilizes the standard progression of comic panels to highlight how this wound appears on Roxy. The first panel that shows the damage is a single image highlighting a line from the top of Roxy's head down through her midsection that disappears from view where her arm obscures it. The next panel mimics this line, but instead of showing the actual wound that has separated her into two parts, a closer inspection reveals that the line is actually a panel border. This scene is unique to comics since the image shows exactly what a film frame might (the two halves of the body), but does so in a way that tells the reader that this is part of a larger progression of time and motion. It's a comic-book spin on a filmic trope, much like the film's cinematic reinterpretations of video-game and comic influences. It's also one more example of why both the film and the comic are unique versions of the same story.

One of the most persistent concerns that comes with adapting any comic into a film is the role of sound. A comic is a purely visual work of art, forced to suggest sound through either the content of its images or textual displays such as word balloons and onomatopoeia-infused exclamations like "KPOK" or "POW." Many clever comic-book artists and writers take full advantage of this fact, using the physicality of sound on their pages to interact with the story being played out. It's not a requirement of good comic art or storytelling, but since any comic is going to devote portions of its visual landscape to pure text, those words need to be carefully selected to make the most of their page space. Sound in film is an added layer that accentuates the visual action that's taking place, and while the same can be said about a comic's text, those words must fight for the same real estate as the comic's visuals. It's a much more delicate balance between sight and "sound" and the best comic creators understand this fact. O'Malley certainly does, and time after time he makes intelligent choices about how to deploy sound visually so that it furthers the storytelling. One such instance occurs during Ramona and Scott's first date. The pair is seeking refuge at Ramona's apartment from the sudden snowstorm that hit during their walk, and Ramona suggests some tea to warm up. When Scott asks what flavor options he has, Ramona rattles off a massive list of choices in a word balloon that's noticeably bigger than any other on either the current or preceding page. O'Malley reflects the ridiculous number of teas in Ramona's possession by creating a word balloon that's expansive in the same fashion as her overly large collection of tea. For comparison, the word balloon featuring Ramona's list of teas features forty-two words in total. The second largest word balloon on either of these two pages tops out at sixteen words. The list is nearly three times as large as any other word balloon on the two visible pages. This hefty amount of text in a word balloon isn't a common occurrence either. The balloon isn't big simply because the list is long. In other instances where O'Malley has a larger amount of dialogue to fit into a panel, he breaks up speech into multiple balloons. Not six pages later, Ramona's dialogue is broken up into two chunks in two conjoined word balloons. The first balloon features nineteen words and the second thirteen. That's a total of thirty-two words, and despite the fact that it's ten words shy of the list of teas it still receives multiple word balloons. O'Malley consciously chose to represent the sound of Ramona's speech as a voluminous list, and to do so he gave the text a presentation that breaks from the normal speech patterns of the characters. He created a patch of dialogue that reads in a unique fashion despite the text itself being no different from any of the other standard text being presented to the reader.

Wright, too, finds a way to distinguish this moment in the film, and he does so by layering in a few techniques to highlight the absurdity of the overlong list and capitalize on film techniques. As Ramona heads over to the cabinet, the

Bryan Lee O'Malley uses a large word balloon to evoke the sense of a vast list. From *Scott Pilgrim's Precious Little Life* (July 2004). Art by Bryan Lee O'Malley. Copyright © Bryan Lee O'Malley.

camera cuts to a close-up of Ramona with Scott over her right shoulder. She begins to rattle off name after name in a rapid-fire delivery that's distinctly more affected than any of Ramona's more "natural" dialogue. The camera also holds the shot, not moving an inch, to highlight the protracted and almost practiced nature of Ramona's listing of the teas. Just as the comic utilized a break from the natural pacing of its depiction of dialogue, the film breaks from the natural delivery of the actors' dialogue to showcase the humor in the overlong list. Wright also adds in another aural element to the scene in the form of the tea kettle hissing its alert that the water has reached its boiling point in the background of the rest of the scene's aural design. It's a lot of sonic information, too much to ever properly convey on the printed page, but where O'Malley can load up half of the panel with a visual representation of sound, Wright goes for an aural overload that includes the sound effect of a boiling tea kettle and a song playing on the soundtrack. Mixed in with the unnaturally long shot of Ramona glancing about the cupboard the scene takes on a similar feeling to its counterpart in the comic even though it shares few, if any, of the stylistic techniques that make the comic feel the way it does. Sound is a powerful tool, and though it may not be a component of comics, its absence allows creators in the medium different methods of playing around with that absence in their efforts to tell their stories.

Wright isn't content to solely use sound and its role in the film in a traditional style, however. While the vast majority of the dialogue in his film is standard audible stuff, Wright is willing to take some cues from the comic and its stylistic choices to spin the film's audio in different ways. In the lead-up to Sex Bob-Omb's first public performance in the movie the band is watching their competition's set. Stephen Stills begins freaking out, but since Crash and the Boys are so loud, his dialogue ends up appearing on screen as subtitles. Subtitles are a fairly common occurrence in film, at least in films that feature a foreign language and require translation, but what's unique here is that Wright has intentionally thrown off the sound mix to necessitate these subtitles. Stills is speaking English, so if his dialogue was made a little bit louder the subtitles would be unnecessary, but by softening his dialogue Wright accentuates Stills's breakdown. The music is an oppressive force that's drowning him out as he's attempting to connect with his band mates in the moments leading up to their show. Wright further stylizes the sequence by allowing the subtitles themselves to subtly shift and move on the screen. When Stills asks his band mates "How are we supposed to follow this?" the "follow this?" lingers on the screen, slowly growing bigger in size and pushing out toward the audience. Just as comics can give words physical space on the page, Wright has found a way to create a visual representation of Stills's anxiety and fears through a physical representation of his speech. The subtitles effortlessly mimic his concerns and worries, and even manage to highlight the ways that the other members of the band are relating to him. In the final moments of Stills's breakdown he charges toward Scott, who is gazing not at the other band but the two girls he is dating concurrently, completely unaware of Stills. Stephen ends up begging Scott to stop, simply standing there, and as he does so his subtitles become partially obscured by Scott's head, further showcasing just how little attention Scott is paying to him. The words displaying on screen are a desperate plea from a character who is being completely ignored by Scott, and even worse, they're obfuscated by the very character to whom the pleas are directed. It's the perfect visualization of Scott's selfish nature and it's a technique that Wright wisely gleaned from O'Malley's books and comics in general.

While a film can use subtitles as much as it wants, Wright cleverly deploys them only in a few sparing moments such as the one we've just discussed where it doesn't draw too much undue attention. Since comics speech consists of written words, comics can have a much easier time transitioning in and out of stylistically adventurous depictions of text than a film might. Take, for example, a similar scene where Scott falls into his own world while ignoring the conversations taking place around him. In a series of four panels Scott munches on a plate of food while the dialogue progressively pixelates and eventually becomes unintelligible around him. Wright's film never truly obfuscates Stills's words or intentions from the viewers in this scene. It's a subtler evocation of Scott's self-focused nature, whereas O'Malley's depiction of Scott completely isolates him from the outside world. O'Malley funnels the reader into that same place as the dialogue becomes completely unreadable and the panels themselves show nothing but Scott and his nachos. The world outside of Scott's mind ceases to exist for those few panels. O'Malley replicates that feeling of insulation and isolation in the reader by cutting off any sound or visual that isn't directly related to Scott eating his nachos, as the dialogue is totally unintelligible, but it's telling that O'Malley includes three repetitions of "munch" in one panel. Sound isn't gone from Scott's world entirely, just the sound that's unrelated to what he's doing, and O'Malley beautifully showcases just how easily comics can create subjectivity through their visual representations of sound.

It all comes back to the fact that comics are a medium out of time. Anyone hoping to successfully adapt a comic into a film has to grapple with moving something that can only suggest and imply the passing of time into a medium that is wholly focused on unstoppable forward movement. That notion is succinctly encapsulated in a single scene featured in both the comic and the film just after Scott finally breaks things off with Knives and rides a public bus back home. Scott's thoughts initially dwell on Knives and the anguish he's caused her, but ultimately they turn toward Ramona and the happiness he's found with her. Both O'Malley and Wright find exceedingly impressive ways to frame this transition, and both do so in ways that showcase the storytelling capabilities of their respective media. O'Malley stages the scene on two neighboring pages with layouts that are just shy of symmetrical. In fact, if all the images from the panels are removed on the first page and the layout rendered upside down, it becomes the layout for the second page. It's a perfect, barely perceptible reflection of Scott's changing mindset as he moves from upset to happy. While it might not have meaning devoid of the context the images provided, O'Malley has exploited the fact that readers will see the entirety of the two pages as they read and he has presented a visual accompaniment to the material contained within those panels. Similarly, the layout allows O'Malley to position Scott's musings on the two women in his life in locations on the page that aren't read consecutively but are taken in as a whole when the pages are viewed all at once. The panels create a ring of sorts around the center of the page, and in that center are four images, one of Knives, then two of Scott, and a final image of Ramona. Those images fit in with the standard top-to-bottom, left-to-right reading order of most comics, but they also function as the centerpiece of the entire spread. The two pages are about Scott's move from Knives to Ramona, and that movement is encapsulated in these four panels as Scott somberly dwells on Knives and then perks up when he remembers the girl he's moving on to. It's exactly what comics do so well; they create a linear story but due to the nature of the medium, they also create images and tell that story in a way that isn't necessarily bound by one image coming before the next.

It's telling, then, that when Wright adapts this scene into a film it becomes very much about images in a specific sequence. Wright focuses almost the

O'Malley stages Scott's bus ride home, during which he thinks of two different women, on two opposing pages. From *Scott Pilgrim Vs. the World* (May 2005). Art by Bryan Lee O'Malley. Copyright © Bryan Lee O'Malley.

entirety of the scene on the four panels that make up the center of O'Malley's layout. Wright retains the establishing shot of the bus rolling down a Toronto city street, but once he shifts inside the bus, the film refocuses into a scrolling series of images that alternate between Scott, Knives, and Ramona. Wright displays the images in such a fashion that they resemble comic-book panels, but the scene still feels essentially filmic as the images are all rolling along the screen at the same time. It lends the scene a fluid sense of momentum that evokes a comic in some ways. The images comingle onscreen since the "panels" that Wright creates don't take up the entire frame. But the images' irrepressible sense of forward momentum, beautifully underscored by the music cue of "Teenage Dream" by the band T-Rex, renders them as filmic. The best example of this shift comes from the way that Wright depicts Scott's changing mental state. O'Malley accomplishes this through tools like page layout, but Wright chooses to showcase Knives slowly fading to black in her panels while Scott in the next panel cheers up and Ramona in the next image fades into view. Comics are certainly able to use techniques like dissolves, but to do so requires multiple panels, as in the way that O'Malley spreads out the dissolving dialogue over the course of four unique images. It's a process that's possible, but not as effortless as it is in film. The comic masterfully strips the scene down to its most basic components, eliminating any dialogue or visual effects save for a final indication of a musical note as Scott exits the bus, focusing instead on the raw power of comics to juxtapose concurrent images.

Film has that same power of juxtaposition, but it generally must do so through cuts and editing rather than placing two images physically next to one another. Here, Wright chooses to do just that. The images slide across the screen, challenging the viewer to take in all that they can before each image disappears from view. The visual flow of the scene is clear. Knives's disappearing act obviously pushes the viewer to the next panel, while Ramona's appearance marks a point where her image becomes the "right" one to be looking at, and Wright handles all this through tools such as motion. He highlights small movements of the characters, removes some from view, and eliminates others off the side of the screen. Even when Wright's film becomes more comic-like in its storytelling style, it's still guiding the viewer through its story in ways that are distinctly filmic.

Wright adapts O'Malley's work consciously with the intention of creating a film that is an authorial adaptation, with its own artistic identity. The film mines its source material to great effect but is never overly precious with the comics or too tethered to them. Wright is a fiercely unique filmmaker and his style shines through even as it's influenced by, and respectful of, the style of O'Malley's original work. Part of this is likely due to O'Malley and Wright's particular styles being well-suited to one another. They both have an abundance of boundary-pushing energy that bounces off the edges of their respective media and pushes them just a little bit further than might be advisable. What ultimately makes *Scott Pilgrim vs. the World* such a successful adaptation is that it's truly a film rather than a comic transplanted to the big screen. Wright understands the medium of film and he never gets too invested in trying to make it conform to the rules of comics, even as he figures out ways to rejigger the medium to reflect the movie's source material. It's a movie infused with comic-book DNA rather than a poorly imagined moving version of the comic. Comic-book films have to do more than simply bring static panels to life; they need to understand just why those panels were static in the first place and what that meant to the story being told. When the images suddenly spring to life, the delicate balance of the work can be thrown off. Wright accomplishes this balance gracefully, and in doing so creates a new and vibrant interpretation of O'Malley's story that's fascinating and exciting in its own right, all while paying homage to the material that spawned it.

To be Continued...

This was not, and could not be, an all-encompassing look at how comics and films converge and diverge aesthetically, but it has hopefully been an enlightening pursuit. The brief look at *Wanted* provided a basic example of how the concept of fidelity does not relate completely to faithfulness when it comes to adapting materials across media. This concept, in turn, became one of the driving forces behind this book as a whole. One of the most important questions dealt with in the first chapter was how films could translate a comic into the medium of film and if it was possible to do so while remaining completely faithful in an aesthetic sense. My preliminary belief was that since the media are separate entities, a completely faithful adaptation would cause problems in terms of storytelling. This turned out to be essentially true, and in each case presented we saw how comics and film shared some similar traits, but ultimately diverged in fundamentally important ways. For some, such as *Watchmen*, which was an admittedly extreme case, this caused more problems than others, but in the end success seemed to be largely intertwined with a willingness to reinvent and repurpose the source material to more effectively bring out the core of the work in the chosen media format.

We began by examining two related, but not directly equivalent works: *Iron Man* and *The Invincible Iron Man*. This gave us a clear view of a comic that attempted to present itself in a cinematic fashion alongside a film that fit comfortably into the mainstream of blockbuster filmmaking. Here we saw how even when a comic or a film attempts to evoke another medium it is still beholden to the pressures and requirements of its own medium. Most notable is that *The Invincible Iron Man* is a "cinematic" comic that seems primarily concerned with replicating "widescreen" aesthetics. There is very little else that implies a cinematic approach, though, prompting the conclusion that while *The Invincible Iron Man* is certainly not a traditional comic in terms of its overt aesthetics, it is still a comic in terms of its fundamentals. The book presents a façade that recalls film but never truly replicates the way that film tells stories, and this is how one medium evokes the other. Even the "cinematic" comic is still a comic, through and through. Next we moved on to examining the two versions of *Sin City*, one in comic form and the other in the form of a film that overtly attempted to recreate the comic aesthetic. In a similar fashion to trends in the works involving Iron Man, we saw that, even as a film attempts to recreate comic stylization, it must do so in uniquely filmic ways if it hopes to effectively tell a similar story. Similarities between the media will always persist, but the unique natures of the media will almost always force stories to change if they hope to be successful as they cross into a different method of storytelling.

The two versions of *Sin City*, as well as the adaptation of *Persepolis*, showcase just how dissimilar the same story can be when it shifts between media. Examining a variety of scenes and how they were presented in both comics and film was useful to point out how the same creator can drastically alter the same basic story to most effectively present it in a different medium. Marjane Satrapi and Frank Miller were the original writers and artists of the comics as well as the co-directors of the films based on their works, so it was safe to say that the two pieces would feature a shared artistic sensibility with their comic-book predecessors. Discovering just how disparate the comics and the films were on an aesthetic level made a strong case for the fact that the two media have two distinct sets of pressures that they exert on storytellers. Seeing how Satrapi and Miller told the same story in two different ways illustrated this point and also showcased how a creator will drastically alter the presentation of content to preserve the effect the content will have. This showed once more that fidelity is an issue of functional equivalency between media rather than blindly copying the original work.

Watchmen helped prove a counterpoint to these adaptations, showing how an overly-faithful approach to translating comics to the medium of film can cause the story to break down. The film wasn't a complete failure, and Snyder most certainly attempted to bring the comic into the world of film, but he lacked the ability to truly get at the core of the work and too often settled for simple re-creation rather than faithful reinvention. That was a problem that director Edgar Wright never faced in his work adapting Bryan Lee O'Malley's *Scott Pilgrim* stories to the big screen. Wright's unique and at times wildly divergent telling of O'Malley's story burst into cinematic life, gleefully playing with motion, sound, and all the tools afforded to film to create a work of art that paid homage to its source as well as its source's own inspirations. This infused the film with video game flourishes, such as subtle sound effects, which the comic was never able to employ, and helped the film hone in on the heart of the story. By doing so, Wright was able to twist and mutate the work without ever losing its core, creating an adaptation that stands beside its source material respectfully without being too beholden to it.

I hope that this book has demonstrated that the adaptation of material from comics to film, and the reverse of this process, is no simple task and one that is not to be taken lightly. Beyond this, I hope to have presented an enlightening look at comics and how they can be just as formally complex as any film might be. The most important issues to arise have revolved around the ways that the audience interacts with comics and film. Film is a much more linear experience since it is able to effectively convey motion and sound, which structures film in a rigid fashion in relation to time and viewer experience. Comics, on the other hand, must deal more heavily with guiding the reader to create a desired experience since they cannot strictly control how the reader moves through the story. They must evoke emotions and feelings with their content while also considering how they will focus a reader's attention in terms of the page and the relationship between panels. Because of this separation, some of the most glaring divisions between comics and film have emerged due to the fact that comics are a purely visual and static medium. Many of the key issues that this book returned to, such as page layouts and how the juxtaposition of panels on a page craft a reading experience, relate to this concept while film can use both motion and sound as tools. Even though comics and film are both visual media, this doesn't imply that a successful adaptation could simply animate a panel and achieve fidelity. Comics are built around the fact that they are visually static, developing an entire language and array of tools to function within a realm that cannot easily dictate time to the reader. Because of this, storytelling must be altered when brought to a medium such as film that is not static. So while panels can certainly be made to move, doing so in a careless fashion will undermine the original intent and craft that made them effective.

In the future, perhaps this division between the media will become less prominent. There was a brief push toward motion comics as a new form for comics to explore in the late 2000s, but those comics tended to combine the worst aspects of comics with the worst aspects of film, and without the budget to pay for high quality voice actors, many felt laughably cheap. Currently, comics are beginning to experiment with the newly burgeoning digital market. Both Marvel and DC are making small forays into the digital-first arena, developing comics that play specifically within the realm of digital screens. This brings a new, more focused form of storytelling to the medium that could develop in interesting and unique ways, completely changing how we read comics. For now, though, film's mastery of time and the way in which the viewer experiences it via the control of motion and sound is still unrivaled by comics. Comics have not yet made this leap, and film still holds the viewer in a way that comics cannot imitate. This isn't anything to lament, since comics also have a rich and varied set of tools available to them that film cannot imitate.

This book is also a response to a large portion of comics criticism which handles comics in a way that largely disregards the formal aspects of the work, favoring an analysis of themes and more literary concerns rather than dealing with how the comic is telling its story. This does not mean that I believe people like Douglas Wolk have no place in comics criticism, or that a purely formal approach to comics is correct. Instead, I hope for a joining of the two, utilizing formal analysis to more concretely analyze and understand the content and thematic concerns of comics. This book has skewed toward the formal aspects of the two media in the interest of focusing on an aspect of film and comics that would effectively represent how the two media differ. Therefore, aesthetics seemed to be the most overt and effective comparison. In doing so I have had to leave behind enormous aspects of each medium. Dealing with issues such as narrative construction, story content, and other areas of both film and comics that don't fall under the purview of aesthetics would have less effectively proven just how much the two media differ, but this does not mean that they should be forgotten. It is my hope that in moving forward from this work, it will be possible for more critics to bring together the two existing extremes of criticism, the formal and the literary, to create a more effective and all-encompassing approach to comics.

About the Author

Logan Ludwig spent his youth immersed in comics, films, video games, and television. When he went to college, those passions only deepened as he pursued a degree in Film Studies from Wesleyan University. After graduation, he continued to work and follow those passions, which has led him to write about all of those media. He is currently a staff member in the Film Studies department at Wesleyan University and writes for Sequart and other publications.

ALSO FROM **SEQUART**

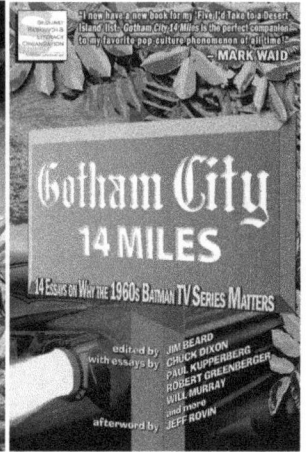

THE FUTURE OF COMICS, THE FUTURE OF MEN: MATT FRACTION'S *CASANOVA*

NEW LIFE AND NEW CIVILIZATIONS: EXPLORING STAR TREK COMICS

GOTHAM CITY 14 MILES: 14 ESSAYS ON WHY THE 1960S BATMAN TV SERIES MATTERS

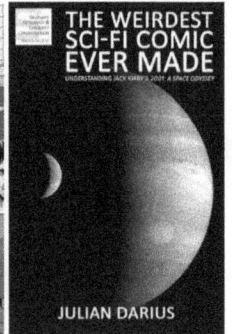

TEENAGERS FROM THE FUTURE: ESSAYS ON THE LEGION OF SUPER-HEROES

IMPROVING THE FOUNDATIONS: *BATMAN BEGINS* FROM COMICS TO SCREEN

MUTANT CINEMA: THE X-MEN TRILOGY FROM COMICS TO SCREEN

THE WEIRDEST SCI-FI COMIC EVER MADE: UNDERSTANDING JACK KIRBY'S *2001: A SPACE ODYSSEY*

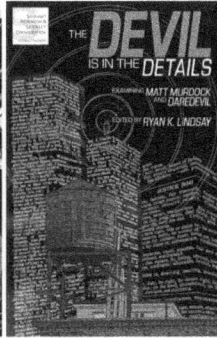

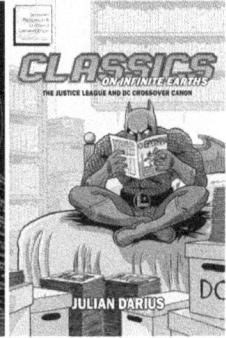

MINUTES TO MIDNIGHT: TWELVE ESSAYS ON *WATCHMEN*
AND THE UNIVERSE SO BIG: UNDERSTANDING *BATMAN: THE KILLING JOKE*
THE DEVIL IS IN THE DETAILS: EXAMINING MATT MURDOCK AND DAREDEVIL
CLASSICS ON INFINITE EARTHS: THE JUSTICE LEAGUE AND DC CROSSOVER CANON

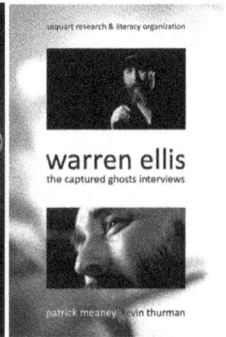

SHOT IN THE FACE: A SAVAGE JOURNEY TO THE HEART OF *TRANSMETROPOLITAN*
KEEPING THE WORLD STRANGE: A *PLANETARY* GUIDE
VOYAGE IN NOISE: WARREN ELLIS AND THE DEMISE OF WESTERN CIVILIZATION
WARREN ELLIS: THE CAPTURED GHOSTS INTERVIEWS

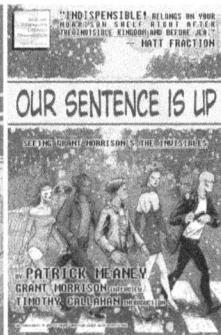

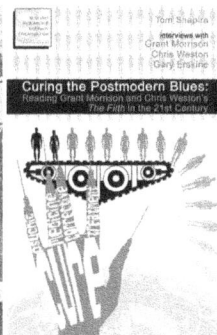

GRANT MORRISON: THE EARLY YEARS
OUR SENTENCE IS UP: SEEING GRANT MORRISON'S *THE INVISIBLES*
CURING THE POSTMODERN BLUES: READING GRANT MORRISON AND CHRIS WESTON'S *THE FILTH* IN THE 21ST CENTURY
THE ANATOMY OF ZUR-EN-ARRH: UNDERSTANDING GRANT MORRISON'S BATMAN

For more information and for exclusive content, visit Sequart.org.

www.ingramcontent.com/pod-product-compliance
Lightning Source LLC
LaVergne TN
LVHW011204080426
835508LV00007B/587